Cosmop...
Meals in...

Also by Richard Ehrlich and published by Robson Books

Cosmopolitan Perfect Pasta

Cosmopolitan Meals in Minutes

by
Richard Ehrlich

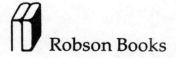

Robson Books

FOR REBECCA AND ALICE

First published in Great Britain in 1992 as *The Cosmopolitan After-work Cookbook* by Vermilion, an imprint of Ebury Press, Random House, 20 Vauxhall Bridge Road, London SW1V 2SA

This edition published in 1997 by Robson Books Ltd, Bolsover House, 5-6 Clipstone Street, London W1P 8LE

Copyright © 1992 National Magazine Company Limited and Richard Ehrlich

The right of Richard Ehrlich to be identified as author of this work has been asserted by him in accordance with the Copyright, Designs and Patents Act 1988

British Library Cataloguing in Publication Data
A catalogue record for this title is available from the British Library

ISBN 1 86105 132 8

Printed by The Guernsey Press Company Limited, Guernsey, Channel Islands

Contents

Acknowledgements 6

Introduction 8

STARTERS AND SNACKS 13

SOUPS 22

MEAT 30

FISH 42

POULTRY 55

PASTA, LENTILS AND RICE 68

VEGETABLES AND SALADS 84

PARTY MENUS 99

PUDDINGS 113

SAUCES, DIPS AND SPICE MIXES 120

Index 125

Acknowledgements

IT WOULD BE IMPOSSIBLE to name all the people who have helped me in my work as Food Editor of *Cosmopolitan*. Here are some of them.

First: my colleagues past and present from *Cosmo*, and especially my editor Marcelle d'Argy Smith. Every cookery writer should receive the unfailing enthusiasm and expert guidance that I have had from her, and from her predecessor Linda Kelsey. After them I must name Rachel Shattock, Liz Gregory, Shirley Saphir, Joan Tinney, Vanessa Raphaelly, Linda Wood, Ruth Farnsworth, Elaine Robertson, Eleni Kyriacou, Tania Unsworth, Wendy Bird, Howard Scott, and Patrizia Diemling.

For advice and information I am indebted to many people, who I hope will forgive me for the bold listing of their names.

Shaun Hill, Gidleigh Park, Chagford, Devon; Sally Clarke, Clarke's, London; Simon Hopkinson, Bibendum, London; Carla Tomasi, Frith's, London; John Burton-Race, L'Ortolan, Shinfield, Berkshire; Antony Worrall-Thompson, 190 Queensgate, London; David Wilby, Rock Island Diner, London; Matthew Fort and Colin Spencer, the *Guardian;* Marian Archer, Diane Lamb and Louise Platt, J Sainsbury; Jenny Fieldgrass; Susan Spencer, Karen Rogers and

Nichola Holgate, Tesco; Vivienne Jawett, Marks & Spencer; Wendy Harries-Jones, the John Lewis Partnership; Katie MacAulay, Oddbins; Rosamund Hitchcock, Biss Lancaster Public Relations; Annie Todd and Vicky Bridges, Darwell Smith Associates; everyone at Alan Crompton-Batt Associates; Sophie Vallejo, Food and Wine from France; Conal Walsh and Lindsay Stewart, Conal Walsh Public Relations; and Richard Guy, The Real Meat Company.

Special thanks are due to Bob Birchenall of B&M Seafoods, London; Jonathan Goodman; and the late Jeremy Round of the *Independent*, who freely spent his time giving advice, information and opinion. For help and encouragement in putting this book together I thank Rowena Webb and Lansing Andolina of Ebury Press, and Helen Southall for her careful attention to the manuscript.

Finally I thank the friends and in-laws who tasted recipes under development, often at an unpleasantly early stage. And very special thanks to my wife Emma Dally; my daughters Rebecca and Alice Ehrlich; and Anne Green and Jenise Hutchinson, without whom nothing would be possible.

Apologies in advance to anyone I've forgotten.

Richard Ehrlich

Introduction

EVERYONE LIKES TO EAT, but few of us have the time or inclination to spend a long time cooking. Fortunately, you don't have to cook elaborately to cook well. After-work cooking is all about producing delicious meals, from fresh ingredients, in little more time than it takes to scramble an egg. This book gives some ideas for how to do just that.

THINK AHEAD

It would be nice if every recipe in this book took 3 minutes to prepare and 4 minutes to cook, but it's no fun limiting yourself to 'instant' recipes. To eat well, and with variety, you sometimes have to spend as much as 20 minutes on preparation and another 20 minutes on cooking. That's the bad news.

The good news is that 20 minutes of preparation and cooking is not as long as it sounds. Turn on the radio; pour yourself a glass of wine or mineral water; take your shoes off and relax. Cooking is an unpleasant chore only if you believe it to be a chore. If you plan your cooking life properly, it will be as easy and as natural as opening a can of soup.

When I say 'plan', what I mean is plan *ahead*. If a recipe seems too time-consuming to bother with just for one or two, think ahead and do some of the preparation in advance, then you can make it easily. And you owe it to yourself to make the small extra effort. Cooking simple but tasty meals is part of treating yourself well.

Shopping

The process of cooking begins not when you get into the kitchen but when you do your shopping. Many of us, when we go into the supermarket or do the rounds of butcher, fishmonger and greengrocer, think, "What am I going to cook tonight?" That's the wrong question. The right questions to ask yourself are: "Can I buy food for today, tomorrow and the day after? Can I make extra sauce tonight and freeze some so I'll have a meal waiting for me next Tuesday? Can I bake an extra potato tonight and mash the leftovers tomorrow?"

Bulk shopping is usually thought of as the province of people with large families and even larger fridges. This needn't be the case. My own fridge is the small size, under waist-high. Yet with careful use of fridge space I can easily store enough food in there for three days' meals. Three days is about the limit, especially as fresh meat and vegetables shouldn't be kept much longer than that. Within those limitations, however, you can do a lot. Let's say you're shopping on Saturday morning for the weekend's food, plus dinner after work on Monday evening. You've got people coming to dinner on Saturday night, but apart from that you'll be buying for two. Here is a menu planner for those three days:

Saturday dinner: Guacamole (see page 20); Roast Chicken (see page 56), steamed vegetables and Perfect Mashed Potatoes (see page 98); fresh fruit

Sunday lunch: Chicken sandwiches
Sunday dinner: Spaghetti alla Carbonara (see page 75), green salad

Monday dinner: Hamburgers 'alla Pizzaiola' (see page 38), green salad

Without going into details about every single item, here are the basics of your shopping: You need a couple of avocados for the Guacamole, a chicken and some vegetables and fruit for the rest of the meal. Chicken and vegetables go into the fridge; fruit into the fruit bowl. Assuming you've got some bread, the sandwiches take care of themselves, being made from leftover chicken. Your packet of pasta goes into the larder, as does the onion; the bacon and mince can sit in the meat drawer of the fridge. Buy salad stuff for two meals; a large lettuce or bag of mixed salad leaves can easily squeeze into the vegetable drawer.

Cooking

In cooking, too, advance planning can make your life much easier. Take the recipe for Roast Chicken (see page 56). It takes about an hour to cook, and needs further resting time. If you're cooking for one or two, this seems a time-consuming extravagance, but in fact you're making three meals at once. If you eat the chicken with one other person, you will have at least half of it left over – more if you eat lightly. The next night you can make Leftover Chicken with Peppers (see page 63) or Sesame Chicken Salad (see page 64), or you could just make some chicken sandwiches.

A different kind of planning is called for once you get in the kitchen. Some of the recipes in this book begin with the words: 'As soon as you walk in the door...'. This isn't a command, but a signal to tired, hungry cooks that some aspect of the cooking takes time; and that if you get it started the minute you get home, you'll eat that much sooner. Ideally, 10 minutes of a meal that takes 20 minutes to prepare should be spent sipping wine and reading the paper.

Advance planning will greatly simplify your cooking life. You'll quickly see that one spell in the kitchen can produce two, three or even four meals – with little extra effort. Many of the recipes in the book can be cooked in advance, while for others, at least part of the preparation can be done ahead of time. I have indicated in the recipes where this time-saving is possible.

HOW LONG DOES IT TAKE?

It's hard to be precise when stating how long a recipe takes. Just as no two ovens are identical, neither are any two cooks. A job that takes a professional 20 seconds might take you or me 5 minutes. However, it is useful to have guidance on preparation and cooking, and the recipes in this book try to provide such a guide. They are not scientific. I don't know how long it takes you to chop an onion; nor do I know whether you have a food processor, or a fan-assisted oven, or someone to help you in the kitchen. All these factors affect your cooking, and they may mean that a recipe takes you 5 minutes more or less than it takes me.

EQUIPMENT

None of the recipes in this book calls for special equipment, but I assume that you own at least one good frying pan, one large casserole, and a saucepan or two. You should also have at least two good knives, one small and one large. Keep them sharp by sharpening *little but often;* get a lesson from a butcher or fishmonger if you don't know how to do it.

The only machines I think every kitchen should have – apart from a cooker, of course – are a blender and a food processor. Blenders are indispensable if you make puréed soups (see page 22). A food processor speeds up many kitchen tasks, from chopping to slicing to mixing. If you don't have one, make this your next major kitchen purchase. Once you have one, you'll wonder how you ever got along without it.

Then there's the question of microwave ovens. I have had one for three years, and I love it dearly. The microwave is brilliant for all sorts of dishes. It can cook without extra fat, so it's great for people who are worried about their weight. It's appallingly healthy, especially as a method of cooking vegetables, because cooking times and nutrient loss are minimal. And it's perfect for after-work cooks, because it's so fast.

Since not everyone has a microwave, I haven't included microwave recipes in this book, though I occasionally point out procedures that can be done either in the microwave or conventionally. If you have a microwave, I hope you use it for more than reheating cups of coffee and convenience foods. If you don't have one, consider getting one. Your kitchen life will be a lot easier.

THE RECIPES

Experimenting is part of the fun of cooking, and all recipes – including those in this book – can be varied according to your tastes and market availability. If you don't have precisely the herbs or vegetables that I specify, use another one. The dish will be just as good, perhaps even better.

Many of my recipes use 'exotic' ingredients. This doesn't mean they are 'authentic' Chinese, Thai or Indian food. Those cuisines are time-consuming when all the rules are followed. But their *flavours* can be incorporated easily into Western-style dishes, and that's what I do. Ethnic variations on standard dishes are perhaps the most fruitful area for home experimentation. For instance, the Cajun Spice Mix (page 124) can be combined with almost any ingredient.

For everyday cooking, it's best to rely on simple combinations of two or three dominant flavours. Using more runs the risk that flavours will battle against one another on plate and palate. Don't let powerful ingredients overwhelm delicate ones, don't experiment for the sake of experimentation, and don't be too ambitious too soon. On the whole, experimentation succeeds best when it proceeds with a bit of caution. Use unusual ingredients to add an accent to your old favourites; don't try to create a whole new language. Most important of all: follow your instincts. The worst that can happen is that you cook a bad dish. The best that can happen? Some wonderful new discoveries.

For the sake of convenience, all the recipes in this book have been calculated to serve four people. It's a simple matter to halve quantities of ingredients to serve two, or double them up to serve eight.

That's all the introduction you need from me. What remains is to look through the recipes, and to enjoy them. After-work cooking can and should be a pleasure.

Starters and Snacks

T HE RECIPES in this chapter are among the most versatile in the book, capable of performing any role in just about any meal. You can make them as a light lunch or dinner for one or two people; as a starter for a dinner party; or as part of an informal weekend brunch. I am particularly fond of serving Spanish-style *tortillas*, either as a main course or as part of a buffet, and baked eggs can fill the same role. But all these dishes are good ones, and all require little preparation and cooking.

Lowish-Calorie Taramasalata

I love taramasalata but hate the calories in all that oil. Here is a less inflationary version using Greek yogurt.

Preparation time: 15 minutes
Cooking time: 2 minutes

150 g (6 oz) white bread, crusts removed
150 ml (6 fl oz) milk
250 g (8 oz) smoked cod's roe
220 ml (7½ fl oz) Greek yogurt

juice of ½ a lemon
black pepper
few sprigs flat-leafed parsley, finely chopped (optional)

Slice bread and soak in milk for 15 minutes. Meanwhile, peel outer membrane from cod's roe and cut into chunks, then chop in a food processor. Squeeze milk from bread and add bread to food processor. Process for 30 seconds, then add yogurt, lemon juice and plenty of black pepper. Process until smooth, then stir in parsley, if using.

Spring Onion Tortilla

Spanish-style *tortillas* are scrambled eggs, cooked without stirring until well set, and served hot or at room temperature. They can be varied endlessly with a wide range of fillings, and they're perfect for parties. For a particularly impressive effect, stack them like a layer cake with varied colours, using onions, red peppers and spinach to get white, red and green *tortillas*. The traditional method of cooking is to turn them after cooking the first side, but I've always found this difficult. My technique is to finish cooking with a blast under a hot grill.

Preparation time: 3 minutes
Cooking time: 20 minutes

3 tbsp olive oil	salt and pepper
bunch of spring onions, coarsely chopped	6 eggs
	1 tsp milk

Heat oil in a medium frying pan and sauté onions for 2 minutes. Sprinkle with salt, cover and cook over a gentle heat for about 10 minutes, until the onion is soft but not coloured. The dish may be prepared ahead to this point.

Beat eggs with milk, season with pepper and pour into pan. Cook for about 7 minutes, until eggs are about three-quarters cooked. Turn on grill to highest heat and finish cooking *tortilla* by grilling for about 3 minutes, until browned all over. The eggs should be just set but still very slightly wet at the centre. Using a spatula, ease *tortilla* away from pan and lift on to a plate. If serving at room temperature, leave to cool, then cover lightly with foil. Cut into portions just before serving.

Sweet Pepper Tortilla

Another *tortilla,* somewhat more elaborate and beautiful to look at than Spring Onion Tortilla (left).

Preparation time: 5 minutes
Cooking time: 20 minutes

1 tbsp vegetable oil
1 tbsp extra-virgin olive oil
3 smallish peppers (1 red, 1
*   green, 1 yellow), seeded and*
*   thinly sliced*

1 medium onion, thinly sliced
1 tsp sweet paprika
¼ tsp cayenne
½ tsp cumin seeds
6 large eggs

Heat both oils in a 20-cm (8-inch) frying pan (preferably non-stick) and add peppers, onion and seasonings. Mix well and cook over a low heat, stirring frequently, for about 10 minutes, until softened. Beat eggs and pour into pan. Cook for about 7 minutes, until eggs are about three-quarters cooked. Turn on grill to highest heat and finish cooking *tortilla* by grilling for about 3 minutes, until browned all over. The eggs should be just set but still slightly wet at the centre. Cut into portions and serve hot or at room temperature.

Salad of Marinated and Smoked Salmon

Preparation time: 10 minutes, plus up to 1 hour marinating

100 g (4 oz) salmon fillet,
*   skinned and trimmed*
100 g (4 oz) smoked salmon
3 tsp extra-virgin olive oil

1 tsp red wine vinegar
2 tsp finely chopped fresh chives
salt and pepper
large handful of salad leaves

Cut raw salmon into slices 5 mm (¼ inch) thick and cut smoked salmon into pieces about the same size. Make a vinaigrette dressing by beating together oil, vinegar and half the chives. Season with salt and pepper. Mix one third of the dressing with each of the salmons and marinate in the fridge for up to 1 hour. (Don't worry if you don't have time to marinate. The dish will still taste great.)

Remove salmon from fridge 20 minutes before serving. Just before serving, dress salad leaves with remaining vinaigrette and arrange on plates with salmon. Sprinkle with remaining chives, and serve with brown bread.

Smoked Fish 'Pâté'

Use inexpensive tail-ends of smoked salmon, or smoked mackerel or trout. This is one of my favourite instant starters, and it's low in calories as well. Fresh dill could be substituted for the coriander.

Preparation time: 2–5 minutes, plus up to 2 hours marinating

250 g (8 oz) smoked fish, skin
 and bones removed
250 g (8 oz) cottage cheese
2 tbsp finely chopped spring
 onion

2 tbsp finely chopped fresh
 coriander
2 tbsp finely chopped fresh
 parsley
juice of ½ a lemon
salt and black pepper

Chop fish coarsely by hand or in a food processor, then add cottage cheese and continue to chop and mix until smooth and well blended. Add onion, herbs and lemon juice, plus plenty of black pepper and salt to taste. If possible, leave in the fridge for a couple of hours so the flavours can mellow before serving.

Thai-Style Steamed Eggs

Good as a starter, or for a quick lunch or supper.

Preparation time: 10 minutes
Cooking time: 5–10 minutes

6 large eggs
2 tbsp stock or water
75 g (3 oz) cooked pork or
chicken, finely chopped
(optional)
2 spring onions, finely chopped

6 sprigs fresh coriander, finely
chopped
2 shallots, chopped or 2 tbsp
chopped onion
1 tbsp Thai fish sauce
1 tsp black pepper

Bring some water to the boil in a wok or steamer. Break eggs into a shallow heatproof dish and beat lightly, then add remaining ingredients and mix well. Place dish in steaming vessel and steam for 5–10 minutes, until just cooked. Serve immediately with rice.

Ceviche

Ceviche is raw fish marinated in lemon or (preferably) lime juice so that the acid 'cooks' the fish. This is an excellent starter or light main course. It must be made in advance, but then there's nothing more to do. If you know you'll be getting home late one evening, make it the evening before and your supper will be ready when you walk in the door. A slice of good bread, a tomato with olive oil, and you're ready to start eating!

Preparation time: 10 minutes, plus up to 24 hours marinating

450 g (1 lb) white fish or
mackerel, skinned
juice of 3 limes or 2 lemons
(about 100 ml/4 fl oz)
1 large or 2 small fresh green
chillies, seeded and finely
chopped

1 small onion or 3 spring onions
(about 50 g/2 oz), finely
chopped
⅛ tsp ground cumin
⅛ tsp ground coriander
3 tbsp tomato juice (optional)
black pepper
1 large tomato

Cut fish into chunks or slices about 1 cm (½ inch) thick and put pieces in a small, deep glass or ceramic bowl with lime or lemon juice, chillies and onions. Season with cumin, coriander, tomato juice (if using) and black pepper. Stir well and leave to marinate for a minimum of 4 hours and a maximum of 24 hours. Just before serving, seed and dice tomato and mix with fish. Serve with brown bread.

Note: This recipe calls for less citrus juice than is usually used. If you like a sharper flavour, use twice the amount of lime or lemon juice.

Baked Eggs

Baked eggs (*oeufs en cocotte* in French) are an under-appreciated treat. Perfect for a quick supper, light weekend lunch, or as a starter for a dinner party, they're a doddle to make and you can use any topping you like. Try sliced mushrooms (raw or sautéed in butter), finely diced mixed peppers and onions, chunks of smoked fish, or bacon and herbs, as in this recipe.

Preparation time: 3 minutes
Cooking time: 6–10 minutes

2 rashers streaky bacon, rinded
1½ tbsp softened butter
4 eggs

black pepper
1½ tbsp chopped mixed fresh
  herbs

Preheat oven to 230°C (450°F, gas 8) and boil a kettle of water. Lightly grill or fry the bacon and chop or crumble into small pieces. Smear four ramekin dishes with butter, break one egg into each and season with black pepper.

Put ramekins in a roasting or baking tin and pour in boiled water to come about halfway up the sides of the ramekins. Bake for 6–10 minutes, until eggs are set but still runny on top. (Cook longer if you don't like runny yolks.) Sprinkle on herbs and eat with a piece of toast. (Taste before adding salt, as the bacon will be salty.)

Bruschetta

Bruschetta is just an Italian version of toast but, like all simple ideas, it gets transformed by the inventiveness of Italian cooks. Serve it as a starter, a nibble with drinks or a light lunch. There's no need for a proper recipe, because this dish can be made with any topping you fancy. Those listed below are some of my own favourites. As you will see, *bruschetta* is just a vehicle for your imagination.

Preparation time: 1 minute
Cooking time: 30 seconds–30 minutes, depending on topping

slices of good bread

Grill, barbecue or roast bread slices in a very hot oven, until crisp and golden. While the toast is very hot, add your chosen topping and serve at once. Choose from the list below or use your own imagination!

Toppings

a cut clove of garlic, rubbed over the surface of the bread, followed by a dribble of olive oil and a sprinkling of fresh herbs;

fresh beef tomatoes, sliced and sprinkled with basil;

sun-dried tomatoes and mozzarella, both cut into small dice;

roasted red peppers (see page 88), cut into strips and sprinkled with thyme;

anchovies and Feta cheese, again with a dribble of olive oil

Avocado with Creamed Smoked Salmon

This would be an indulgent lunch or starter just for yourself or for a dinner party. Use cheap smoked salmon off-cuts to save money. Note that the cream is actually smetana, which has a fat content of about 10 per cent only. You may use single cream if you wish, but it's a little more fattening and lacks the tang of smetana.

Preparation time: 3 minutes

100–250 g (4–8 oz) smoked
  salmon pieces
4 shallots or spring onions, finely
  chopped
4 tbsp smetana or fromage frais

4 small avocados, preferably the
  rough-skinned Hass variety
juice of 1 lemon
salt and pepper

Cut salmon into thin shreds. Mix salmon and shallots or onions with smetana or *fromage frais* and set aside. Peel and stone avocados and mash or finely chop. Mix immediately with lemon juice and spread out on four plates. Top with salmon mixture and season with salt and pepper. Serve immediately.

Guacamole

Preparation time: 10 minutes, plus up to 1 hour marinating

1 tbsp cumin seeds
4 ripe avocados, preferably the
  rough-skinned Hass variety
3 large ripe beef tomatoes,
  skinned, seeded and finely
  chopped

3 tbsp finely chopped fresh
  coriander
2 small green chillies, seeded
  and finely chopped
2 cloves garlic, finely chopped
4 tbsp extra-virgin olive oil
salt and pepper

Briefly cook cumin in a dry frying pan, just until it starts to release its lovely fragrance. Grind in a mortar or coffee grinder and set aside.

Cut avocados in half and remove stones. Scoop out the flesh and roughly mash it in a large bowl. Add cumin and remaining ingredients and mix well. Cover tightly and leave to stand for no more than an hour. If you like it hotter, add more chilli or chilli sauce very sparingly. Serve with bread, or with raw vegetables (crudités) and pitta bread for dipping.

Melted Stilton Sandwiches

An instant hot lunch, or even a starter for an informal dinner party. This is just as good with slightly stale bread.

Preparation time: 1 minute
Cooking time: 1–5 minutes

8 slices good white bread
250 g (8 oz) Stilton cheese
3 tomatoes, thinly sliced

1½ tbsp chopped mixed fresh
  herbs
4 tsp butter

Make four sandwiches with the bread, cheese, tomatoes, and herbs, pressing down hard to squeeze flat. Spread the outsides of the sandwiches with butter. Heat a non-stick frying pan and cook the sandwiches for about 2 minutes each side, until the bread is browned. Alternatively, put sandwiches one at a time on a plate and microwave at full power for 1 minute.

Soups

MOST PEOPLE LOVE SOUP, and few dishes are easier to make. Begin the soup when you get home, before you change your clothes, feed the cat, etc. By the time you've finished unwinding, your soup will be done. Better still, make your soup well in advance. Do the work on Monday evening and you're all set for Tuesday. And since it takes the same effort to make a gallon or a single bowl, why not cook enough for eight or ten portions? You can freeze the rest. And remember that leftover vegetables gain a new lease of life if added to a basic soup.

In some of the following recipes, I specify that the vegetables should be thinly sliced. For puréed soups you might just as well chop them roughly, which is easy if you have a food processor. Also on the subject of food processors: it's tempting to use them for puréeing soup, but this never produces a fine texture. Use a blender or *mouli-légumes*.

Curried Vegetable Soup

This simple soup can be made with whatever vegetables are available – root vegetables, cauliflower, celery, broccoli, Savoy cabbage. It calls for curry powder, but you can add

any flavouring you want: fresh herbs, a spoonful of tomato
purée, a garnish of garlicky croûtons, or whatever else takes
your fancy. Make lots, and eat it again the next day.

Preparation time: 10 minutes
Cooking time: 30 minutes

50 g (2 oz) butter
675 g (1½ lb) winter vegetables,
  roughly chopped
1 medium potato, peeled and
  thinly sliced
1 medium or 2 small leeks, thinly
  sliced

1 tbsp mild curry powder
2 tbsp finely chopped fresh
  ginger
1 clove garlic, finely chopped
1 litre (1¾ pints) chicken stock
milk or Greek yogurt (optional)

Melt butter in a heavy flameproof casserole and cook
vegetables gently, without browning, for 5 minutes. Add
curry powder, ginger and garlic and cook, stirring, for a
further minute. Pour in stock, bring to the boil and simmer
gently for 30 minutes, until vegetables are soft. Purée in a
blender and add milk or yogurt (if using) to bring soup to
your preferred consistency. Serve hot or cold.

Chtchi

Preparation time: 10 minutes
Cooking time: 15–25 minutes

1 medium 'floury' potato (such as
  King Edward)
450 g (1 lb) cooked spinach
  (fresh or frozen)
3 tbsp butter
1 small onion, finely chopped
1 litre (1¾ pints) chicken or
  vegetable stock

salt and pepper
4 tbsp Greek yogurt
2 hard-boiled eggs, finely
  chopped
2 tbsp finely chopped fresh
  parsley

Boil or microwave potato until just cooked, then peel and
mash. In the meantime, if using fresh spinach, chop finely.
If using frozen, remove from freezer and break up the block
with a sharp knife.

Melt butter in a large saucepan and sweat onion for 2–3
minutes. Add spinach and potato and blend well. Pour in

stock, season with salt and pepper, and cook gently for 5 minutes. Whisk in yogurt and cook for a few more minutes, making sure it doesn't boil. Sprinkle egg and parsley on top before serving.

Vegetable Soup with Mussels

Without the mussels this is an everyday dish. The mussels turn it into a main course for two, or a starter for a small dinner party. Water could be used instead of stock, but the dish would not be so rich in flavour.

Preparation time: 15 minutes
Cooking time: 25 minutes

1 medium onion
1 medium potato
2 medium leeks
3 carrots
25 g (1 oz) butter

1 clove garlic, finely chopped
1 litre (1¾ pints) chicken stock,
* vegetable stock or water*
1 bouquet garni
900 g (2 lb) mussels

Chop vegetables into bite-sized chunks. Melt butter in a stockpot or large saucepan and sweat vegetables and garlic for a couple of minutes. Add stock or water and bouquet garni and simmer for 15–20 minutes, until just tender.

In the meantime, clean mussels, discarding any that are open or cracked. Put mussels in a saucepan with 3–4 tbsp wine or water, cover and cook for 5 minutes. Discard any mussels that do not open, and strain the cooking liquid into the soup. Add the remaining mussels to the soup and cook very gently for 2 minutes more. The soup may be enriched with double cream or *crème fraîche*.

Cabbage Soup with Almonds

Preparation time is even shorter if you have a food processor.

Preparation time: 5–10 minutes
Cooking time: 30–35 minutes

50 g (2 oz) slivered almonds
25 g (1 oz) butter
450 g (1 lb) green cabbage
  (about ½ small cabbage),
  finely sliced
1 small potato, peeled and thinly
  sliced

½ medium onion, coarsely
  chopped
1 bay leaf
475 ml (16 fl oz) stock
salt and pepper
600 ml (1 pint) milk
juice of ½ a lemon

Toast almonds to a light golden brown in a dry frying pan, then set aside. Heat butter in a large saucepan and sweat cabbage, potato and onion with bay leaf for 3 minutes. Add stock, season with salt and pepper, and simmer gently for 25–30 minutes, until cabbage is soft. When you're ready to serve, stir in milk and heat gently, making sure soup doesn't boil. Stir in almonds and lemon juice and serve.

No-Cook Bloody Mary Soup

Make sure the juice and vegetables are cold when you make this soup to minimise the chilling time. Allow an hour in the freezer if the ingredients haven't been chilled to start with.

Preparation time: 5 minutes, plus 20 minutes chilling

450 g (1 lb) ripe tomatoes,
  peeled, cored and seeded
2 stalks celery, coarsely
  chopped
2 small spring onions, coarsely
  chopped
small handful fresh parsley,
  coarsely chopped

750 ml (1¼ pints) tomato juice
1 tbsp soy sauce
1 tbsp Worcester sauce
4–6 drops Tabasco
salt and pepper
4 tbsp vodka (optional)

Put all ingredients, except the vodka (if using), in a blender and blend for about 40 seconds, until smooth. Chill in the freezer for 20 minutes. If using vodka, mix it into the soup just before serving.

No-Cook Cucumber Soup

Preparation time: 5 minutes, plus 20 minutes chilling

1 clove garlic, coarsely chopped
3 tbsp wine vinegar or sherry
  vinegar
1½ large cucumbers, peeled
450 g (1 lb) Greek yogurt

4 tbsp finely chopped fresh mint,
  chives or dill
salt and pepper
1 spring onion, finely chopped, to
  garnish

Soak garlic in vinegar. Cut 12 paper-thin slices from one cucumber and set aside. Grate remaining cucumber and combine with yogurt and herbs. Season with salt and pepper. Stir well and chill in the freezer for 20 minutes.

Just before serving, strain vinegar into soup and mix well. Garnish soup with slices of cucumber and a sprinkling of spring onion.

Cream of Watercress Soup

A standard soup perked up with lime. Use lemon if you can't get lime. This soup is just as good cold as it is hot.

Preparation time: 5–10 minutes
Cooking time: 30 minutes

one 2.5 × 5-cm (1 × 2-inch)
  piece lime rind
25 g (1 oz) butter
3 bunches watercress, coarsely
  chopped
1 medium potato, peeled and
  coarsely chopped

2 spring onions or 1 small onion,
  finely chopped
900 ml (1½ pints) chicken or
  vegetable stock
225 ml (8 fl oz) single cream or
  Greek yogurt

Blanch lime rind in boiling water for 2 minutes, then drain, dry well and chop finely. Gently heat butter in a large saucepan and stir-fry watercress, potato, lime rind and onion for 1 minute. Add stock, bring to the boil and simmer for about 30 minutes, until soft. Purée soup in a blender and return to saucepan. If serving chilled, allow to cool and refrigerate. Just before serving, stir in cream or yogurt.

Carrot Soup with Ginger and Spring Onion

This soup may be made well in advance and reheated just before serving. It may also be served cold. For a creamier soup, stir in milk or Greek yogurt.

Preparation time: 5 minutes
Cooking time: 35 minutes

2 spring onions
450 g (1 lb) carrots, thinly sliced
1 large baking potato, peeled
  and thinly sliced
1 large clove garlic, finely
  chopped

one 2.5-cm (1-inch) cube fresh
  root ginger, peeled and finely
  chopped
1 litre (1¾ pints) chicken or
  vegetable stock
salt and pepper

Cut off green parts of spring onions and reserve. Finely chop white parts and put in a large saucepan with all remaining ingredients. Bring to the boil and cook gently, partly covered, for 30 minutes or until all ingredients are very soft.

Purée soup in a blender, return to saucepan and reheat. Before serving, season well with salt and black pepper. Finely chop green parts of spring onions and use ½ tsp as a garnish for each bowl.

Lemon Broth with Rice

This simple soup adds sparkle to stock, especially if made from stock cubes.

Preparation time: 2 minutes
Cooking time: 20–25 minutes

1 litre (1¾ pints) chicken or
  vegetable stock
long-grain rice to fill a measuring
  jug to the 175-ml (6-fl oz) mark

small handful fresh parsley or
  coriander, finely chopped
juice of ½ lemon
1 tbsp extra-virgin olive oil
salt and pepper

Put stock in a saucepan with rice. Bring to the boil and cook at a moderate heat, uncovered, for 20–25 minutes, until rice is soft. Add parsley or coriander, lemon juice and olive oil, and season to taste with salt and pepper. Mix well and eat immediately.

Simple Chinese Mushroom Broth

This can be made with either dried Chinese black mushrooms (available from Chinese supermarkets) or fresh shiitake mushrooms.

Preparation time: 5–15 minutes
Cooking time: 10–15 minutes

4–6 dried Chinese black
  mushrooms or 100 g (4 oz)
  shiitake mushrooms
900 ml (1½ pints) chicken stock

1 tsp soy sauce
1 small spring onion
1 tsp sesame oil

If using dried mushrooms, soak them in a bowl of hot water for 10–15 minutes, until they lose all trace of stiffness. Squeeze gently to dry them, cut out stems, and slice the caps 5 mm (¼ inch) thick. If using fresh mushrooms, just wipe them clean and then trim and slice as for dried mushrooms.

Put stock, soy sauce and mushrooms in a small saucepan. Bring to the boil, turn down heat and simmer for 10–15 minutes. In the meantime, cut spring onion into thin disks.

When soup is ready, stir in spring onion and sesame oil, and serve immediately.

Variations

This delicate soup can be made more substantial by adding thinly-sliced beef or chicken for the final 2 minutes of simmering.

Tomato Soup with Basil Croûtons

You could skip the croûtons and serve this soup with Italian bread, such as *focaccia* or *ciabatta*.

Preparation time: 10–15 minutes
Cooking time: 35–45 minutes

15 g (½ oz) butter
1 small onion (about 50 g/2 oz), chopped
1 clove garlic, chopped
½ small red chilli (dried or fresh), seeded and chopped
one 800-g (28-oz) can Italian plum tomatoes

50 g (2 oz) long-grain or Basmati rice
1 tsp mixed dried herbs
1 tbsp tomato purée
salt and pepper
2 tbsp extra-virgin olive oil
2 slices good white or wholemeal bread
4 leaves basil, finely chopped

Gently heat butter in a large saucepan and cook onion, garlic and chilli for 3–5 minutes, until soft but not coloured. Coarsely chop tomatoes and add, with their juice, to the saucepan. Put in rice, herbs, tomato purée, and salt and pepper. Bring to the boil, then turn down heat and simmer gently for 30–40 minutes, until tomatoes are soft and the soup well thickened. Purée in a blender. (The soup may be prepared ahead to this point.)

When ready to serve, bring soup to a gentle simmer. Heat oil in a frying pan. Cut bread into 2-cm (¾-inch) cubes and fry for 30–60 seconds, turning several times, until golden. Remove and sprinkle with basil. Ladle soup into bowls, top with croûtons, and serve. If soup seems too thick, add a little water or stock.

Meat

A LOT OF PEOPLE nowadays avoid red meat. Surveys by *Cosmo* show that around 15 per cent of readers are vegetarians and 44 per cent eat less red meat or only white meat or fish. But that leaves many people who do eat red meat, and I am not ashamed to admit that I'm one of them. No single food, whether it's steak or chips or ice cream, is intrinsically bad for you. If you eat a balanced diet, with fat and sugar kept to a minimum, and fruit, grains and fresh vegetables eaten every day, you will be eating well. Red meat has a place in that diet if you're so inclined.

Nearly all the recipes in this chapter are easily adapted so they can be made with a different type of meat from that specified in the recipe. 'Instant' Chilli (see page 33) can be made with pork or lamb as well as beef. My Japanese-Style Beef Rolls (see page 36) could be made with lamb cut from the leg. The Lamb and Leek Stir-Fry on page 40 could be made, not only with all the meats, but with chicken as well. And while there are no recipes for it here, do look out for the farmed venison which has become widely available in supermarkets and better butchers. It has a strong but not overpowering flavour which most meat-eaters go wild for.

Steak *Frites*

Utterly simple once you've mastered it. Use sirloin or rump, and baking potatoes. I find a wok is best for frying the potatoes.

Preparation time: 5 minutes
Cooking time: 10 minutes

vegetable oil, for deep frying   olive oil, for brushing
4 large baking potatoes, peeled   salt
4 steaks, each about 1 cm
  (½ inch) thick

Heat oil in a saucepan, wok or deep fryer. Trim potatoes and cut into even lengths 5–9 mm (¼–⅜ inch) thick. When oil has reached 180°C/350°F (hot enough to brown a cube of fresh bread in 30 seconds), put in potatoes. Fry for 2–3 minutes, until they feel squishy but are not cooked. Remove and drain. Bring oil back to same temperature.

Brush steaks lightly with olive oil and fry or pan-grill over a high heat. It's hard to be precise about timing, but cook for about 2 minutes for rare, 3 minutes for medium-rare and 4 minutes for well-done. The only sure test is to cut one steak open.

When steaks are a minute or two from being done, plunge *frites* back into hot oil. Test after 1 minute; they shouldn't take more than 2 minutes on the second frying. When done, remove from the oil and sprinkle with salt. Serve immediately with the steaks.

Quick-Braised Pork Chops with Garlic and Red Peppers

This could be made just as well with steaks, lamb chops, or even venison steaks. The cheapest and most flavoursome pork chops are the so-called 'spare rib chops'.

Preparation time: 2 minutes
Cooking time: 15–20 minutes

4 red peppers, seeded
2 tbsp olive oil
4 thick pork chops
2 cloves garlic, finely chopped

450 ml (¾ pint) stock or water
4 sprigs fresh or 8 tbsp dried
*   rosemary*
salt and pepper

Slice red peppers into 5-mm (¼-inch) strips. Heat oil in a large frying pan that has a lid. When really hot, put in pork chops and fry quickly for about 1 minute each side, until seared.

Turn down heat immediately and add garlic and peppers. Add stock or water and rosemary, cover and cook over a low heat for 10–15 minutes. Season with salt and pepper, and serve with potatoes or turnips and French beans or a mixed salad.

Stir-Fried Lamb with Radicchio and Chicory

Preparation time: 5 minutes
Cooking time: 4 minutes

450 g (1 lb) lean lamb from leg,
*   loin or shoulder*
325 g (12 oz) radicchio
325 g (12 oz) chicory
4 tbsp good olive oil

4 tbsp strong chicken stock
2 tbsp dry white wine
1 tsp balsamic vinegar
salt and pepper

Slice lamb about 3 mm (⅛ inch) thick and tear radicchio and chicory into small pieces. Heat half the oil in a wok or large frying pan until smoking, then briskly stir-fry lamb for 1 minute. Remove to a bowl.

Add remaining oil to pan and stir-fry vegetables for 1 minute. Return lamb to pan and add stock and wine. Stir-fry for 1 minute, add vinegar and mix ingredients thoroughly. Season to taste with salt and pepper, then serve immediately with rice.

'Instant' Chilli

Chilli should really cook for a long time over a low heat, but this isn't an option for hungry after-work cooks. This recipe is a compromise for a cold, wet, winter's evening. For more fire, add more chillies. Freezes well.

Preparation time: 5–10 minutes
Cooking time: 30 minutes

3 tbsp corn or sunflower oil
1 large onion, finely chopped
1 stalk celery, finely chopped
2 small red chillies, seeded and finely chopped
2 cloves garlic, finely chopped
1 tsp cumin seeds

1 tsp dried oregano
675 g (1½ lb) shredded or minced beef, pork or lamb
4 tbsp tomato purée
600 ml (1 pint) stock or water
432-g (15.2-oz) can red kidney beans, drained

Heat oil in a flameproof casserole, add vegetables, chillies and garlic, and stir-fry with cumin and oregano over a medium heat for 2 minutes. Add meat and continue frying, stirring frequently, for about 5 minutes, until it loses its colour.

Add tomato purée and stock or water to meat, and mix well. Bring to the boil and boil vigorously for 10 minutes. Add kidney beans and cook for another 10 minutes.

Serve with boiled rice or pitta bread plus your choice of: grated Cheddar or Gruyère cheese; sliced cucumber, celery and lettuce; Greek yogurt or *fromage frais*.

Note: To make this recipe by slower, more traditional means, simmer meat and vegetables over gentle heat for 1 hour before adding beans. As the dish is so much better when reheated, try making it in large quantities the night before people are coming to dinner. That way, you'll save yourself trouble the next night.

Quick-Braised Lamb with Herbes de Provence

Shoulder of lamb is cheaper than leg and just as flavoursome. Get the butcher to cut the meat into chunks if you haven't bought it pre-cut. Rice may be substituted for the spuds if you add about another 300 ml (½ pint) liquid. Excellent reheated.

Preparation time: 5–10 minutes
Cooking time: 1¼ hours

2 tbsp olive oil
½ a boned shoulder of lamb
  (675–900 g/1½ –2 lb),
  cut into 2.5-cm(1- inch)
  chunks
1 large onion, quartered
2 cloves garlic, halved

1½ tsp dried herbes de Provence
600 ml (1 pint) stock or water
50 ml (2 fl oz) dry red wine
2 large leeks
450 g (1 lb) carrots
450 g (1 lb) small potatoes,
  peeled

Heat oil in a flameproof casserole and brown meat on all sides. Add onion, garlic, herbs, stock or water and wine. Bring to the boil and cook over high heat for 30 minutes.

Cut leeks and carrots into 5-cm (2-inch) lengths and add to casserole with potatoes. Cook for another 30 minutes, then skim cooking juices and serve. No other vegetables are needed.

Sausages in a Nest of Cabbage

This simple recipe sounds precious but it's real peasant stuff – hearty, warming and delicious. If the sausages are very fatty, grill them first instead of browning in the pan.

Preparation time: 15 minutes
Cooking time: 15–20 minutes

50 g (2 oz) butter
1 Savoy cabbage, shredded
1 clove garlic, finely chopped
1 sprig fresh rosemary or 1 tbsp
  dried
1 tsp vegetable oil

8 of your favourite sausages
225 ml (8 fl oz) beef or chicken
  stock
3 tbsp dry white wine
salt and pepper

Melt butter in a wide, shallow, flameproof casserole or lidded frying pan and sauté cabbage, garlic and rosemary over medium-high heat for 5 minutes. Remove from the pan and set aside. (This may be done well in advance, even the night before.)

Wipe out the pan, put in the oil and heat. Add the sausages and cook over high heat until brown on all sides. (Alternatively, grill under a fierce heat while the cabbage is cooking.)

Remove sausages from the pan and pour off excess fat. Return cabbage to the pan and bury sausages in it. Add stock, wine and salt and pepper, and scrape the bottom of the casserole to loosen any browning residue. Cover and cook over medium heat for 15–20 minutes. If necessary, moisten the cabbage with more stock during cooking.

Oven-Fried Steak

Frying or grilling steak produces clouds of smoke. This smokeless alternative is a beef-lover's dream. While it finishes cooking you can do other things.

Preparation time: 1 minute
Cooking time: 20–30 minutes

4 beef fillet, sirloin or rib steaks, each about 5 cm (2 inches) thick
salt and pepper

Preheat oven to 240°C (475°F, gas 9). Heat a frying pan with no fat for 5 minutes over the hottest heat. Pat the steaks dry with kitchen paper towels and season with salt and pepper. Slap into the pan and leave for 1 minute, until browned. Turn and brown the other side for another minute. (This may be done hours or even a day in advance.)

Put steaks in a roasting tin and roast at the top of the oven. For medium-rare, fillet will take 15 minutes, rib and sirloin about 30 minutes. Allow 2 minutes more or less if you like beef medium or rare. Cover the meat with foil and leave to rest on top of the cooker or in another warm place for 15–20 minutes before eating.

Japanese-Style Beef Rolls

Preparation time: 10–15 minutes
Cooking time: 2–4 minutes

4 thick or 8 thin spring onions
4 tbsp soy sauce
2 tbsp sake

one 450-g (1-lb) piece of well-
trimmed beef fillet or sirloin
black pepper
corn oil, for brushing

Cut off most of the green part of the spring onions and quarter or halve them lengthways into 16 pieces. Put in a bowl with the soy sauce and *sake* and leave to marinate. Meanwhile, slice beef into 16 pieces of roughly the same thickness. (This is easier if the beef is well chilled or partially frozen.) Press the slices with your fingertips to flatten them, and season with pepper.

Remove the spring onions from the marinade, reserving the marinade. Roll each slice of beef tightly around a spring onion piece, as if rolling a cigarette. If spring onions protrude beyond the ends of the meat, trim off excess.

Preheat grill to highest heat. When it is very hot, brush the grill rack with corn oil and the beef rolls with marinade. Grill the rolls for 2–4 minutes, turning once. Do not overcook. Brush again with the marinade before turning and before serving. Serve with *sake* or Japanese beer.

Note: The beef rolls may also be barbecued or cooked in a well-oiled grill pan.

Hamburgers with Style

V. .iether you're eating alone or with friends, a good burger is hard to beat. Here is the basic technique for cooking your burger, followed by three ways of jazzing it up to make an extra-special meal. I would happily serve any of these burgers to my friends.

Some people mix flavourings into the hamburger patties. I prefer to add any flavourings afterwards, though 1 tbsp Worcester sauce per burger is an acceptable addition. The best way to buy mince is to buy a whole piece of beef – braising steak or chuck is best – and to ask the butcher to mince it to order. If you can't do that, buy the best mince in the shop.

Preparation time: 1 minute
Cooking time: 6–12 minutes

450–550 g (1–1¼ lb) minced   salt and pepper
    beef   ½ tbsp vegetable oil (optional)

Form the beef into four neat patties that are no more than 4 cm (1½ inches) thick. If you're grilling the burgers, preheat the grill for 3–4 minutes, until it is very hot. Season the patties with salt and pepper and grill for 4–6 minutes per side, depending on how well done you like your burgers.

To fry the burgers (my preferred method), put the oil in a frying pan and heat over medium heat for 1 minute. Now turn the heat up to high, leave for 30 seconds, then put in the seasoned burgers. Cook for 3–4 minutes per side (frying cooks meat faster than grilling).

Variation

Cheeseburgers: Add very thin slices of cheese (Cheddar, Gruyère and Parmesan are my burger favourites) immediately after turning. If frying, the cheese will melt better if you cover the pan for a minute or two.

Hamburgers 'alla Pizzaiola'

'Alla Pizzaiola' is a classic Italian way of serving beef with a tomato sauce. If you can't get ripe tomatoes, use a 400-g (14-oz) can of Italian plum tomatoes. You will need to fry your burgers to make this dish.

Preparation time: 2 minutes
Cooking time: 10–20 minutes

1 tbsp extra-virgin olive oil
450 g (1 lb) fresh ripe tomatoes,
　skinned and roughly chopped
4 small cloves garlic, crushed
1 tbsp chopped fresh oregano or
　basil or 1 tsp dried

salt and pepper
½ tbsp vegetable oil
4 uncooked hamburgers (see
　page 37)

Heat oil in a large frying pan and add tomatoes, garlic, herbs and salt and pepper to taste. Cook for 5 minutes over medium heat, then remove to a bowl and wipe out the pan.

Add vegetable oil to pan and heat over a medium heat for 1 minute. Turn heat to high for 30 seconds, then add burgers and cook for 2 minutes each side. Pour the tomato mixture over the burgers, cover and continue cooking over a high heat for 3–5 minutes.

Hamburgers with Instant Wine Sauce

How to turn hamburgers into something special with the minimum of effort. Perfect for using up what's left of a bottle of red wine.

Preparation time: 1 minute
Cooking time: 10–15 minutes

½ tbsp vegetable oil
4 uncooked hamburgers (see
　page 37)
1 small onion, finely chopped

225 ml (8 fl oz) red wine
handful fresh parsley, finely
　chopped
salt and pepper

Heat oil in a large frying pan and cook burgers as in recipe on page 37. When burgers are done, remove them to a heated platter or four plates and keep warm.

Turn the heat up under the frying pan as high as it will go and add onion and wine. Bring to the boil, stirring constantly to scrape up the residue stuck to the pan, and boil rapidly until the wine has reduced in volume by about half. Stir in parsley and season to taste, then pour over the burgers and serve immediately.

Hamburgers with Taco Trimmings

Tacos make a great DIY meal, and the same principle can be used with burgers. No quantities are given for this recipe because the choice and amount of toppings are entirely up to you. Serve on bread or rolls, and warn your friends that they're sure to make a terrible mess!

Preparation time: 20–30 minutes
Cooking time: 6–12 minutes

uncooked hamburgers (see
    page 37)
vegetable oil, for frying
mature Cheddar cheese, grated
Cos lettuce, shredded
green peppers (seeded) and
    cucumbers, sliced
sour cream or Greek yogurt
Tabasco and Worcester sauce

cooked dried or canned kidney
    beans, drained and roughly
    mashed
avocado, mashed and mixed
    with lemon juice, or
    Guacamole (see page 20)
Tex-Mex Salsa (see page 123)
bread or rolls, to serve

Grill, fry or barbecue the burgers as in the recipe on page 37. Serve with a selection of trimmings and let your guests pile on their own choice. Serve on bread or rolls.

Lamb and Leek Stir-Fry

The combination of lamb and leeks is a delicious one, but
this dish could also be made with beef or pork. If using pork,
choose from leg, loin or shoulder. If using beef, only good-
quality steak, such as rump, will do.

Preparation time: 5 minutes
Cooking time: 10 minutes

*250 g (8 oz) lean lamb from leg,
loin or shoulder
1 tbsp soy sauce
1 tbsp dry sherry or dry white
wine
juice of ½ a lemon*

*1 clove garlic, finely chopped
250 g (8 oz) leeks (preferably
small ones)
1 tbsp vegetable oil or extra-
virgin olive oil*

Trim fat from meat and cut into 1-cm (½-inch) thick slices.
(Don't worry if they're not all the same size, as long as
they're about the same thickness.) Put meat slices in a
small bowl. Mix soy sauce, sherry or wine, lemon juice and
garlic, and pour over meat. Leave to marinate.

Meanwhile, cut the leeks in half lengthways, then into
5-cm (2-inch) pieces. Heat oil in a large frying pan over a
medium-high heat and stir-fry leeks for 5 minutes. (Don't
worry if they blacken a little bit – the black bits taste delicious.) Now turn heat up very high and add lamb with its
marinade. Continue cooking, stirring constantly, for 3–5
minutes, until lamb is just cooked. Serve at once with bread
or boiled rice.

Toad in the Hole

The hint of curry powder adds pizzazz, but can be omitted.

Preparation time: 5 minutes
Cooking time: 30 minutes

*125 g (5 oz) plain flour
¼ tsp salt
1 tsp mild curry powder
(optional)*

*1 large egg
300 ml (½ pint) milk
8 good sausages (about
450 g /1 lb)*

To make the batter, sift flour, salt and curry powder into a large bowl and beat the egg in with a wooden spoon. Add the milk bit by bit, stirring steadily, until the mixture is perfectly smooth. Leave to rest for 30 minutes.

Meanwhile, preheat oven to 200°C (400°F, gas 6). Put sausages in a frying pan with little or no extra fat and fry until browned all over. Drain off fat and place in a buttered baking dish measuring about 15 × 20 cm (6 × 8 inches). Pour in the batter and bake at the centre of the oven for about 25–35 minutes, until the batter is nicely brown. Serve with a salad or some stir-fried cabbage.

Bacon and Eggs with Fresh Herbs

If you have bacon and eggs in your fridge, you need never go without a good, quick meal. (See also Spaghetti alla Carbonara, page 75.) This ultra-simple dish takes minutes to prepare. Use good ham if you prefer.

Preparation time: 3 minutes
Cooking time: 3–5 minutes

8 rashers streaky bacon (smoked or green), rinded
8 large eggs

4 tbsp chopped mixed fresh herbs (such as parsley, dill, coriander, chives, tarragon)
black pepper

Slice bacon into thin shreds. Put in a non-stick frying pan and heat gently to soften, then turn heat up to medium and fry for 2–4 minutes, until cooked the way you like it.

Beat eggs with herbs and some black pepper. Turn up heat under pan and pour in eggs. Cook, stirring constantly, until the eggs are done the way you like them. Eat immediately with a slice of good brown bread.

Fish

FISH HAS BENEFITTED from the trend towards lighter eating, yet many people are intimidated by the prospect of trimming and filleting: a 1991 survey found that few consumers knew what to do with a whole fish. The supermarkets are clearly aware of this, as you will see from their ranges of trimmed fish portions. But don't be put off by whole fish: the smaller ones especially (red mullet, trout, mackerel) are easy to prepare and cook. You can ask the fishmonger to cut off the head for you, and after that it's no more difficult (or messy) than dealing with fillets or steaks.

I haven't included many recipes for shellfish, as they can be expensive. But the Seafood Ragoût with Lemon Grass (see page 49) is a real delight for a special occasion, and mussels, which I cook with ginger and spring onion (see page 47) are still relatively inexpensive. Look out for fish with unfamiliar names like ling, huss and gurnard; some of them are excellent. And when buying fish, look for a clean, 'un-fishy' smell, bright, clear eyes (if the fish has its head on), and a bright look to the flesh.

One final word about fish: please patronise your local fishmonger. A good fishmonger is an expert, and can tell you not only about the fish itself but about how to cook it. The people who work in supermarkets may lack that expertise.

Simon Hopkinson's Poached Cod with Salsa Verde

Poaching the fish with the skin on helps hold its shape. Simon Hopkinson, chef of London's Bibendum restaurant, serves this with lentils (see page 80). A piece of good brown bread would do.

Preparation time: 5 minutes
Cooking time: 5 minutes

750 ml (1¼ pints) fish stock or 500 ml (17 fl oz) white wine and 225 ml (8 fl oz) water
4 cod fillets, skin on, each about 150 g (6 oz)

Salsa
large handful fresh parsley, finely chopped
1 clove garlic, finely chopped
2 tbsp capers, finely chopped
juice of ½ a lemon
4 tbsp extra-virgin olive oil

Heat stock or wine and water in a large flat pan. While it's heating, make the *salsa*. Mix parsley, garlic, capers and lemon juice with oil. When stock is barely simmering, add cod and poach for 3–5 minutes. Drain, remove skins and serve with *salsa*.

Fish Roll-Ups with Spinach and Spring Onion

Preparation time: 5 minutes
Cooking time: 5–10 minutes

4 large flat spinach leaves, central ribs removed
4 tsp dry white wine or vermouth
4 tbsp finely chopped spring onion

4 sole or plaice fillets, skinned
black pepper
lemon wedges, to serve (optional)

Plunge spinach into boiling water for 45 seconds. Drain and pat dry.

Sprinkle wine or vermouth and spring onion over one side of fillets and grind on pepper. Lay spinach flat on fish and roll into neat 'cigar' shapes. Trim edges of spinach if necessary. Place on a heatproof plate or in a bowl and steam for 5–10 minutes.

If you like, boil strained cooking juices rapidly for a minute to reduce, then pour over fish. Otherwise, just serve with lemon wedges.

To microwave: Place fish roll-ups in a small heatproof glass bowl. Cover tightly with clingfilm and cook at full power for 5–6 minutes.

Blackened Fish

Use any fish fillets as long as they're not more than 2.5 cm (1 inch) thick. The technique also works beautifully with lamb chops and steak, but cooking times will have to be adjusted. Before you begin, open the windows, turn on the extractor fan and temporarily disconnect the smoke detector, if you have one, as this cooking method produces a lot of smoke. Omitting the oil ('dry' blackening) will produce less smoke.

Preparation time: 2 minutes
Cooking time: 10 minutes

4 small fish fillets, skinned   1 recipe Cajun Spice Mix (see
6 tbsp vegetable oil   page 124)

Place a heavy frying pan or grill pan over the highest heat your hob will produce and leave it there for 5 minutes. In the meantime, brush fish with oil and rub both sides with spice mix.

Put fish in pan and cook for 2 minutes each side; avoid moving fish, except when turning, as it may break up. If serving at room temperature, leave to cool on a platter and get out of the kitchen while the smoke clears!

Mackerel in White Wine

Preparation time: 2 minutes, plus 20 minutes marinating
Cooking time: 15 minutes

1 small onion, very thinly sliced
1 medium mackerel, filleted and
* skinned*
1 bay leaf, crumbled
2 tbsp chopped mixed fresh
* herbs (such as thyme,*
* tarragon, dill and chives)*

75 ml (3 fl oz) dry white wine or
* vermouth*
3 tbsp fish stock or water
salt and pepper

Put onion in a non-stick frying pan and lay fish on top. Add remaining ingredients and spoon over fish. Leave to marinate in a cool place for at least 20 minutes, spooning marinade over fish occasionally.

Cover the pan loosely with foil and cook over a medium-low heat for about 15 minutes, spooning the liquid over the fish two or three times. If the liquid is cooking away, add a little more wine, vermouth or water.

This dish can also be cooked in the oven. Put fish in a baking or gratin dish and cook at 190°C (375°F, gas 5) for 20–25 minutes. It's even better, and faster, cooked in the microwave (see below).

Serve the fish hot or at room temperature, with French bread.

To microwave: Cover the dish (which must be non-metallic) with clingfilm and microwave at full power for 3½ minutes.

Squid with Three Peppers

Squid is ideal for this dish, but uncooked prawns or fillets of a firm-fleshed fish, such as monkfish, may be used instead.

Preparation time: 10–15 minutes
Cooking time: 7–10 minutes

450 g (1 lb) squid, uncooked
  peeled prawns or fish fillets
1 green, 1 red and 1 yellow
  pepper, seeded
1 small green chilli, seeded
  (optional)
3 tbsp corn or peanut
  (groundnut) oil

salt and pepper
1 tsp cumin seeds
1 tsp tomato purée
3 tbsp strong fish or chicken
  stock
2 tbsp cream, crème fraîche or
  Greek yogurt

If using squid, clean it and cut into bite-sized pieces. If using frozen prawns, thaw completely. If using fish, skin fillets and cut into strips or discs about 1 cm (½ inch) thick. Cut peppers into long shreds, and chilli (if using) into thin slivers.

Heat half the oil until very hot in a wok or frying pan. Add peppers, season with salt and pepper, and stir-fry for a few minutes, until softened but still quite crunchy. Remove from pan.

Heat rest of oil in pan and add cumin and squid, prawns or fish. Stir-fry for 2 minutes, then return peppers to pan and continue cooking for 1 minute. Add tomato purée and stock, and season with salt and pepper. Toss well for another minute or so. When fish is cooked, stir in cream or yogurt and serve immediately.

Mussels with Ginger and Spring Onion

The technique here is similar to that used for classic mussel dishes such as *moules marinières*.

Preparation time: 10–15 minutes
Cooking time: 5 minutes

900 g (2 lb) mussels
5 spring onions
4 tbsp corn or peanut
  (groundnut) oil
one 2.5-cm (1-inch) cube fresh
  ginger, peeled and cut into fine
  shreds

1 clove garlic, finely chopped
2 tbsp soy sauce
2 tbsp Chinese rice wine or dry
  sherry
1 tsp cornflour (optional)

Clean mussels, discarding any that are open or cracked. Cut one spring onion into slivers and reserve for garnish. Cut remaining onions into fine shreds.

Heat oil until very hot in a wok or frying pan and add ginger, shredded spring onions and garlic. Toss well for a few seconds, then add mussels. Stir-fry for 2 minutes, then add soy sauce, wine or sherry and cornflour (if using). Stir well to mix, cover and cook for 2–3 minutes. Remove and discard any mussels that have not opened.

Transfer mussels to a large bowl, garnish with reserved spring onion and serve with bread or rice to soak up the cooking liquid.

Grilled Cod with Herb Crust

Preparation time: 5 minutes
Cooking time: 5–10 minutes

1 tbsp finely chopped fresh
  parsley
1 tbsp finely chopped fresh dill
1 tbsp softened butter
salt and pepper

2 tbsp dried breadcrumbs
4 cod fillets, each about
  150 g (6 oz)
vegetable oil, for brushing

Preheat a baking sheet or roasting tin under the grill. Mix herbs with butter, salt and pepper and breadcrumbs, and spread evenly over skinned side of fish.

When grill is really hot, remove baking sheet or roasting tin and brush with a little oil. Place fish, skin side down, on oiled area and grill under a fierce heat for 5–10 minutes, until fish is just cooked. It will not need turning. Serve immediately with new potatoes and steamed French beans.

Red Mullet with Wilted Watercress

This dish can be microwaved or steamed, and eaten cold, warm or hot. If you make it on Thursday night it will be ready for Friday dinner. Another small fish (or fish fillets) may be used instead of red mullet.

Preparation time: 5–10 minutes
Cooking time: 10–15 minutes

2 bunches watercress	1 lemon
4 tbsp single cream or Greek yogurt	salt and pepper
	4 red mullet, cleaned

To make the watercress purée, wash watercress, drain and remove thick stems. Blanch in boiling salted water for 3 minutes and drain well, then chop or purée in a blender. Mix with cream or yogurt. Season with a squeeze of lemon juice, salt and pepper, and return to the saucepan.

Rub fish with cut lemon, sprinkle with pepper and lay in a heatproof glass dish. If steaming, cook over boiling water in a wok or steamer for 5–10 minutes, until fish is tender.

When fish is ready, gently reheat the watercress purée but do not let it boil. Serve the fish with new potatoes or bread and a salad, with the watercress purée on the side.

To microwave: Puncture the eyes of the fish, arrange them in the dish with tails towards centre, and cover tightly with clingfilm. Cook at full power for 5–6 minutes. Pierce the clingfilm and let stand for 2 minutes.

Seafood Ragoût with Lemon Grass

This is a little fiddly for a quick evening meal but well worth the effort. Use scallops, monkfish, squid, prawns, langoustines and other firm-fleshed fish, such as salmon or halibut. Everything can be done well in advance, and the cooking takes minutes.

Preparation time: 15–20 minutes
Cooking time: 5–6 minutes

1 shallot or spring onion, finely chopped
1 clove garlic, finely chopped
2.5-cm (1-inch) piece lemon grass, finely chopped
1-cm (½-inch) cube fresh ginger, peeled and finely chopped
25 g (1 oz) butter
100 ml (4 fl oz) dry white wine

100 ml (4 fl oz) fish stock
325 g (12 oz) mixed seafood (see above), cut into bite-sized pieces
2 tbsp finely chopped fresh coriander
2 tbsp single cream or fromage frais (8 per cent fat)

To make the sauce, cook shallot or onion, garlic, lemon grass and ginger gently in butter for 2 minutes. Add wine and stock (or extra wine if you don't have fish stock). Boil rapidly until reduced by about three quarters. (Remove from heat if cooking in advance.)

Six minutes before serving, heat sauce over a gentle heat. Add uncooked seafood, mix well and cook gently for 5 minutes. If using any cooked seafood, add after 4 minutes. Stir in coriander and cream or *fromage frais* and serve with rice and salad.

John Dory with Orange Cream

Don't worry – it's not real cream. Use any flat fish if JD is not available.

Preparation time: 5 minutes
Cooking time: 10–15 minutes

3 oranges
salt and pepper
4 John Dory fillets, each
  125–150 g (5–6 oz)

150 ml (6 fl oz) crème fraîche *or*
  Greek yogurt

Slice one orange into 12 segments and reserve for garnish. Squeeze juice from remaining oranges. Boil juice rapidly over a high heat until reduced by three quarters, then season with salt and pepper and set aside. Season fish with salt and pepper and steam for 4–8 minutes, until tender.

While fish is cooking, gently reheat orange juice and whisk in *crème fraîche* or Greek yogurt, taking care not to let it boil. When fish is cooked, spoon sauce on to four warmed dinner plates. Place a fillet on each, garnish with three segments of orange and serve immediately.

Quick-Baked Fish Fillets with Wine and Mushrooms

Use any flat fish, such as plaice or sole, or tail portions of cod or haddock. This dish could be cooked just as well in a covered frying pan, reducing the cooking time to 3–4 minutes, or in a steamer.

Preparation time: 10 minutes
Cooking time: 10–15 minutes

4 fillets of flat fish
salt and pepper
250 g (8 oz) mushrooms, thinly
  sliced

4 tbsp dry white wine
2 tsp olive oil

As soon as you walk in the door, preheat oven to 230°C (450°F, gas 8). Place fish in a lightly buttered baking dish and season with salt and pepper. Scatter mushrooms over fish, then sprinkle or brush on wine and oil. Bake at the top of the oven for 10–15 minutes, until fish is just opaque.

Fish Fillets 'Pipérade'

Pipérade is a Basque scrambled egg dish made with peppers, onions and, sometimes, tomatoes. The vegetables can also be used as a topping, and can be prepared well in advance.

Preparation time: 5 minutes
Cooking time: 10–15 minutes

2 tbsp olive oil
1 medium onion, thinly sliced
2 peppers, preferably 1 red and
  1 yellow, seeded and thinly
  sliced

1 clove garlic, finely chopped
4 fish fillets (such as cod,
  haddock or salmon)
4 tbsp dry white wine
salt and pepper

Heat oil in a large frying pan and sauté onion for 2 minutes over a medium-high heat. Add peppers and garlic and continue cooking for about 3 minutes, until peppers are softened but still firm to the bite. If preparing in advance, allow to cool, cover and refrigerate until needed. Remove from fridge 30 minutes before cooking.

Put the fish fillets in a frying pan or roasting tin which will hold them in one layer. Sprinkle fish with wine and season with salt and pepper. Spread *pipérade* evenly over fish and cover loosely with foil. Put pan on a low heat and cook very gently for 4–5 minutes, until fish is just opaque inside and *pipérade* is heated through. Serve hot or at room temperature.

Marinated Salmon

The salmon must be very fresh, since it is served raw. Your fishmonger can do much of the preparatory work for you. This would make a luxurious main course for four people or an elegant dinner-party starter for six to eight people. The dish would also be good made with halibut or with smoked Scottish salmon.

Preparation time: 15 minutes, plus 15 minutes–2 hours marinating

675 g (1½ lb) salmon fillet, skinned
4-cm (1½ -inch) cube fresh root ginger, peeled and coarsely chopped

2 tbsp extra-virgin olive oil
juice of 1 lemon
salt and pepper

Use tweezers to extract any small bones remaining in the fillet. Cutting diagonally with a very sharp knife, cut fish into slices no more than 5 mm (¼ inch) thick. Arrange in overlapping layers on a large platter. Put chopped ginger in a garlic press and squeeze out juice. (You need about 2 tbsp.)

Mix ginger juice, oil and lemon juice and brush gently all over the fish, then season with pepper and a little salt. Cover platter tightly with clingfilm and refrigerate until you're ready to eat. It will be delicious after 15 minutes, but can easily be marinated for up to 2 hours. Serve salmon with buttered brown bread.

Fish Steaks on a Bed of Carrots

Fish and carrots make a terrific pair. This simple but delicious dish can be made with cod, haddock, salmon – just about any steak that's available. Use ruby port or dry white wine if you don't have any dessert wine.

Preparation time: 3–5 minutes
Cooking time: 10–15 minutes

2 large or 4 small carrots
25 g (1 oz) butter
4 tbsp dessert wine
1 tsp dried herbes de Provence
  or mixed dried herbs

4 fish steaks, each 2.5–4 cm
  (1–1½ inches) thick
salt and pepper

Slice carrots as thin as you can get them; this is easiest using the slicing disc on a food processor.

Melt butter in a large frying pan and add carrots, stirring to coat evenly with butter. Pour in wine, add herbs and cook very gently, stirring regularly, for 5–10 minutes, until the carrots are soft but still a tiny bit crunchy.

Season fish on both sides with plenty of salt and pepper and place in the pan. Cover and cook for 2–3 minutes on each side, until fish is just done. Serve immediately with bread, boiled potatoes or rice.

Cotelettes Pojarski

An ultra-simple dish, originally made with chicken. Pojarski was a Russian innkeeper.

Preparation time: 15 minutes
Cooking time: 6–8 minutes

100 g (4 oz) white bread, crusts
  removed
milk
325 g (12 oz) skinned fish fillets
  (such as haddock, cod or
  whiting)
3 tbsp finely chopped fresh parsley

salt and pepper
dried breadcrumbs or cornmeal,
  for coating
40 g (1½ oz) clarified butter
  (see **Note** overleaf)

Put bread in a bowl, cover with milk and leave to soak. Finely chop fish. Squeeze most of milk out of bread and mix well with fish and parsley. Season with salt and pepper. Form into four oval cakes and coat lightly with breadcrumbs or cornmeal. Heat butter in a frying pan and fry *cotelettes* for 3–4 minutes on each side, until brown. Serve piping hot.

Note: To clarify butter, heat gently in a small saucepan until half melted. Turn off heat and leave to melt completely. Skim off white bits (whey protein), then pour out butter, leaving sediment and water in bottom of pan. This is easier to do with 100 g (4 oz) or more of butter. Clarified butter will keep in the fridge for a couple of weeks.

Poultry

I LOVE ANYTHING WITH WINGS, and I'm not alone: chicken has become one of Britain's favourite foods. With the wide range of products available – not just whole birds but chicken pieces, chunks, even slices – poultry is a natural choice for after-work cooks.

Whatever you do with your bird, make sure it's a free-range chicken. The term free-range is subdivided into 'free-range', 'traditional free-range', and 'free-range total freedom'. As a general rule, birds in the latter two categories are best.

Some game bird recipes are also included in this chapter. Among other birds, duck is a personal favourite of mine. Most supermarket chains sell not only whole ducks but a variety of joints. I prefer to buy a whole bird, but it's easier to buy duck in pieces. Farmed quail is another tasty treat, widely available from supermarkets. It looks very impressive when you have guests coming to dinner, but its size also makes it a good choice for one or two eaters. Guinea fowl, which is like a strong-tasting chicken, is well worth seeking out. In game season, don't miss grouse, pigeon, pheasant and wild duck. Though not as easily found as guinea fowl, their flavour is incomparable.

Baked Chicken Wings

Chicken wings may well be the tastiest part of the bird –
and they're also the cheapest. The coating may be used as a
marinade if you wish; brush on and leave for 1–2 hours or
overnight.

Preparation time: 10 minutes
Cooking time: 20–25 minutes

900 g (2 lb) chicken wings
75 ml (3 fl oz) soy sauce
50 ml (2 fl oz) tomato purée
2 tbsp Worcester sauce

3 tbsp dry sherry
4 tbsp corn or sunflower oil
1 clove garlic, crushed or finely
   chopped

As soon as you walk in the door, preheat oven to 230°C
(450°F, gas 8). Divide chicken wings at joints, saving tips
for stock, and place in a single layer on a baking sheet. Mix
remaining ingredients and brush generously over wings.
Bake in upper third of oven for about 20 minutes, until
done, turning and basting three or four times. Serve hot or
at room temperature.

Basic Roast Chicken

The chicken cavity can be seasoned in any way you like. My
recipe is nothing more than a suggestion.

Preparation time: 5 minutes
Cooking time: 50–55 minutes

1.3–1.7 kg (3–3½ lb) ovenready
   chicken
2 cloves garlic, chopped
large handful fresh parsley,
   chopped

1 tsp chopped fresh tarragon or
   1 tsp dried
25 g (1 oz) butter (optional)
salt and pepper

If possible, remove chicken from fridge 1 hour before
roasting. Preheat oven to 230°C (450°F, gas 8).
    Put garlic and herbs inside chicken cavity. Place chicken,
breast-side down, on a rack in a roasting tin and smear
back with butter (if using). Season with salt and pepper and

roast for 30 minutes. Turn chicken over and roast with breast-side up for 20–25 minutes more. Allow to stand for at least 15 minutes before carving.

Chicken 'Boulangère'

This is loosely based on a French dish using lamb cutlets. You'll need a large non-stick pan with a lid. If you're making it for two, try it with a 'spatchcocked' poussin, available ready-prepared from some supermarkets.

Preparation time: 10 minutes
Cooking time: 30–35 minutes

450 g (1 lb) 'waxy' potatoes (such as Maris Bard), peeled
4 chicken breasts or 8 thighs
2 smallish leeks, cut into 5-mm (¼-inch) disks

3 tbsp chicken stock
3 tbsp dry white wine
1 tsp chopped fresh tarragon
salt and pepper

Cut potatoes into 5-mm (¼-inch) slices. If using chicken breasts, cut them in half. Heat a large non-stick lidded pan to medium-hot and sauté chicken for about 3 minutes each side, until very lightly browned. Remove and set aside.

Pour off most of fat from pan and add potatoes, preferably in one layer. Cook over a fairly high heat for 5 minutes, turning once, until potatoes are nicely browned. Lay chicken and leeks on top, pour on stock and wine, sprinkle with tarragon and season with salt and pepper. Cover and cook over a medium heat for 20 minutes, until chicken is just cooked. The chicken juices will pervade the potatoes, giving a lovely flavour and aroma.

Stir-Fried Chicken with Ginger and Spring Onion

This is a greatly simplified version of a Chinese favourite.

Preparation time: 15 minutes
Cooking time: 3–5 minutes

4 chicken breasts or legs,
  skinned and boned
4 tbsp vegetable oil
8 thin slices fresh root ginger,
  peeled and finely chopped

4 spring onions, cut into shreds
2 cloves garlic, finely chopped
salt and pepper
4 tbsp dry sherry
4 tbsp soy sauce

Cut chicken into thin slices or small chunks. Heat oil until very hot in a wok or frying pan and add chicken, ginger, spring onions and garlic. Season with salt and pepper and stir-fry for 2–4 minutes, until just cooked. Turn off heat, mix in remaining ingredients and serve immediately with plain boiled rice.

Cajun Smothered Chicken

This is a good, easy dish for impromptu dinner parties. It's equally good if you're dining alone or *à deux,* since the leftovers are delicious.

Preparation time: 15 minutes
Cooking time: 35–45 minutes

4 chicken breasts or legs (halved
  if legs)
½ quantity Cajun Spice Mix (see
  page 124)
salt
3 tbsp vegetable oil
1 red and 1 yellow pepper,
  seeded and thinly sliced

1 medium onion, thinly sliced
1 clove garlic, finely chopped
1 stalk celery, cut into shreds
225 ml (8 fl oz) chicken stock
2 tbsp finely chopped fresh
  parsley
2 spring onions, finely chopped

Sprinkle chicken with spice mix and salt. Bring oil to a high heat in a large flameproof casserole and brown chicken quickly on all sides. Turn down heat and add peppers, onion, garlic and celery. Pour on stock, cover casserole and cook gently for 30–40 minutes. Just before serving, stir in parsley and spring onions. Serve with rice or beans and a green salad.

Baked Chicken with Yogurt

Preparation time: 5 minutes
Cooking time: 40–50 minutes

3 tbsp vegetable oil
2 medium leeks, white parts
  only, thinly sliced
4 medium carrots, thinly sliced
4 medium turnips, thinly sliced
1 large onion, thinly sliced

1 clove garlic, cut into fine
  shreds
1 tsp cumin seeds (optional)
4 chicken breasts or legs
4 thin slices lemon
8 tbsp Greek yogurt
100 ml (4 fl oz) chicken stock

As soon as you walk in the door, preheat oven to 230°C (450°F, gas 8). Heat oil in a roasting tin until medium-hot, add vegetables and garlic and sweat for 1 minute. Add cumin (if using) and continue to cook, stirring frequently, for 4 minutes more. (Moisten with water if necessary to keep vegetables from sticking.)

Put chicken pieces in tin with a slice of lemon underneath each one. Spread yogurt generously over each piece; it should be at least 5 mm (¼ inch) thick.

Pour stock over vegetables and put tin in oven. Cook, basting with juices every 10 minutes, until chicken is done (about 30 minutes for breasts, 35 minutes for legs). Serve with rice or noodles.

La Fausse Poule au Pot

Classic *poule au pot* is made by poaching a whole stuffed chicken in stock. This inauthentic version is somewhat daintier. Use homemade stock if possible.

Preparation time: 15 minutes
Cooking time: 35 minutes

2 large leeks	2 litres (3½ pints) chicken stock
4 large carrots	6 cloves garlic
4 chicken breasts or legs	250 g (8 oz) French beans

Cut leeks lengthways into thin strips and cut strips into 7.5-cm (3-inch) lengths. Prepare carrots in the same way. If preferred, fry chicken pieces on skin side only until a pale golden brown. (All this may be done well in advance.)

Bring stock to a gentle boil with garlic in a large saucepan. Add chicken and cook for 10 minutes, then add leeks and carrots and cook for 20 minutes more. Finally, put in beans and cook for another 5 minutes.

To serve, put a portion of each vegetable on four warmed plates with the chicken, and serve with a little stock, which may be reduced or enriched with cream or *crème fraîche*. Alternatively, serve the classic *poule au pot* accompaniment of *Sauce Sorges*, a thick vinaigrette with parsley, shallots, chives and hard-boiled egg yolks.

Hot and Sour Chicken with Citrus Shreds

Preparation time: 20 minutes
Cooking time: 10 minutes

pared rind of ½ lemon	4 medium carrots, cut into shreds
pared rind of ½ orange	3 tbsp dry white wine
2 chicken breasts (about 450 g/ 1 lb), skinned, boned and cut into chunks or shreds	4 tbsp good chicken stock
4 tbsp corn or peanut (groundnut) oil	1 sprig fresh tarragon or 1 tsp dried (optional)

Marinade

2 tbsp lemon juice   1 small clove garlic, finely
1 tbsp soy sauce   chopped
1 tbsp sugar   ½ tsp chilli sauce, or to taste
1 tbsp cornflour   black pepper

Cut lemon and orange rinds into thin shreds about 5 cm
(2 inches) long. For marinade, mix together all ingredients.
Blend thoroughly with chicken and leave to marinate for
20 minutes, if liked.

In a large frying pan or wok, heat 1 tbsp oil to a high heat.
Stir-fry lemon and orange rind shreds for 30–60 seconds,
until slightly wilted. Remove from pan and drain. Heat
2 tbsp oil to a high heat and stir-fry chicken (with marinade)
for 2–3 minutes, until nearly cooked. Remove and drain. Add
rest of oil and stir-fry carrots for 2–4 minutes, until nearly
cooked.

Return chicken to pan and add wine, stock and tarragon
(if using). Stir-fry for another minute or two, until chicken
is just cooked and carrots cooked but still crunchy. Remove
to a serving plate and scatter the citrus shreds on top. Serve
immediately with rice.

Chicken with Mushrooms and Garlic

Omit the butter for an ultra-low-cal main course.

Preparation time: 10 minutes
Cooking time: 50 minutes

8 cloves garlic   250 g (8 oz) shiitake or common
4 chicken breasts   mushrooms, sliced
1 tbsp chopped fresh parsley or   225 ml (8 fl oz) stock or water
   basil   1 spring onion, sliced
                                                  25 g (1 oz) butter

As soon as you walk in the door, preheat oven to 180°C
(350°F, gas 4). Cook garlic in boiling water for 20 minutes,
then drain.

Lay chicken breasts in a single layer in a small casserole or baking dish. Sprinkle on herbs, garlic, mushrooms and stock or water. Add spring onion and dot with butter. Cover and cook in the oven for 30 minutes. Great served with boiled rice and green beans.

Chicken with Indian Spices

Preparation time: 5 minutes
Cooking time: 35–40 minutes

1 tsp each fenugreek, cumin,
* coriander and fennel seeds*
2 green cardamom pods
black pepper

2 tbsp vegetable oil
4 chicken breasts or legs
1 large onion, sliced

As soon as you walk in the door, preheat oven to 230°C (450°F, gas 8). Crush coriander and cardamom with a rolling pin and mix with remaining spices, black pepper and half the oil. Rub into chicken and, if there's time, leave to marinate for a while. (This can easily be done the night before you plan to eat the dish; the flavour will benefit from overnight marinating.)

Lay half the onion slices in a roasting tin. Put in chicken, lay remaining onion slices on top and brush with remaining oil. Bake for 35 minutes (breasts) or 40 minutes (legs). Serve with rice and vegetables of your choice.

Marinated Chicken Thighs

Another dish that will benefit from being marinated overnight, so start the day before, if possible.

Preparation time: 5 minutes
Cooking time: 20 minutes

juice of 1 lemon
1 fresh chilli, seeded and finely
* chopped, or 1 tbsp chilli sauce*
1 tsp coriander seeds, lightly
* crushed*

1 clove garlic, crushed
1 tsp dried tarragon
1 tbsp vegetable oil
8 chicken thighs

Combine all ingredients, except chicken, in a bowl large enough to hold the chicken. Add chicken, stir to coat, and leave to marinate as long as possible.

Preheat oven to 230°C (450°F, gas 8). Put chicken on a non-stick baking sheet and bake for 20 minutes, until just done. Serve hot or warm.

To microwave: Brown chicken thighs first if you wish, then arrange them around the rim of a large plate and cover with another plate. Microwave at full power for 5–8 minutes, until just cooked.

Leftover Chicken with Peppers

Leftover chicken is extremely versatile stuff. I sometimes buy more than I need, then make a leftover dish like this one, to serve with rice or noodles the next day. Remember that the chicken must be cooked for a very short time the second time round. Make sure you heat it right through but don't overcook it.

Preparation time: 5 minutes
Cooking time: 15–20 minutes

½ a roast or boiled chicken (ie 2 quarters), skinned and boned
15 g (½ oz) butter or 1 tbsp olive oil
1 medium onion, sliced
1 clove garlic, finely chopped

1 tsp mixed dried herbs
2 red, green or yellow peppers, seeded and sliced
225 ml (8 fl oz) chicken stock or 100 ml (4 fl oz) water and 100 ml (4 fl oz) white wine

Chop chicken into shreds or chunks. Heat butter or oil in a large saucepan and gently sauté onion, garlic and herbs for 2 minutes. Add peppers and sauté for another 2 minutes.

Add chicken stock or water and wine, bring to the boil, cover and cook for 10 minutes at a very low heat. Add chicken, stir well, cover and cook for another 2–3 minutes, until heated through. Serve immediately with rice or pasta.

Sesame Chicken Salad

Preparation time: 5–10 minutes
Cooking time: 2–30 minutes (depending on whether chicken needs cooking)

4 chicken breasts or legs
  (cooked or uncooked)
1 heaped tbsp peanut butter
1 tbsp peanut (groundnut) oil
1 tbsp soy sauce
½ tsp sesame oil

1 tbsp lemon juice
1 tbsp dry sherry
1 tbsp Dijon mustard
1½ tbsp finely chopped fresh
  ginger
1 tsp sesame seeds

If using uncooked chicken, poach it (preferably in chicken stock) for about 30 minutes, until just cooked. (Save stock for soup.) Put chicken on a plate large enough to hold pieces in one layer, cover with a colander and leave to cool.

Mix together all remaining ingredients, except sesame seeds. Skin and bone chicken and cut into chunks or shreds. Toss with dressing.

Heat sesame seeds in a dry frying pan for a minute or so, until pale golden brown. Sprinkle over chicken and serve.

Provençale Chicken

This can easily be made the night before, and it freezes well.

Preparation time: 15 minutes
Cooking time: 40–45 minutes

3 tbsp extra-virgin olive oil
8 chicken thighs or drumsticks,
  or 4 chicken breasts
1 large onion, coarsely chopped
4 cloves garlic, coarsely
  chopped
1 tbsp chopped fresh thyme or
  1 tsp dried
1 bay leaf

½ can anchovies, chopped
  (optional)
75 g (3 oz) stoned green olives
  or 2 tbsp capers
400-g (14-oz) can Italian plum
  tomatoes, drained and
  coarsely chopped
1 tbsp tomato purée
100 ml (4 fl oz) chicken stock or
  white wine

Heat oil over a medium heat in a flameproof casserole large enough to hold the chicken. Add chicken pieces and cook for a couple of minutes, just long enough to colour the chicken lightly, then put in the onion, garlic and herbs. Fry gently for 2–3 minutes, just until the mixture starts smelling really great.

Add anchovies (if using) to the casserole with olives or capers, tomatoes, tomato purée and stock or wine. Bring to a simmer and cook at a good pace for 30–35 minutes, spooning the sauce over the chicken every 10 minutes or so. The cooking liquid is absolutely delicious.

Honey-and-Spice Roasted Poussins with Sweet and Sour Gravy

This honey coating may also be used for roast chicken.

Preparation time: 5 minutes
Cooking time: 35–40 minutes

3 tbsp clear honey	salt and pepper
1 tsp ground cumin	100 ml (4 fl oz) chicken stock
1 tsp ground coriander	50 ml (2 fl oz) dry white wine
1 tsp ground ginger	50 ml (2 fl oz) red wine vinegar
2 ovenready poussins	or sherry vinegar

As soon as you walk in the door, preheat oven to 230°C (450°F, gas 8). Mix honey with spices and brush half of mixture evenly over backs and legs of poussins. Season well with salt and pepper. Place poussins, breast-side down, on a rack in a roasting tin and roast at the centre of the oven for 20 minutes. Turn poussins over and brush breasts with remaining mixture. Roast for another 15–20 minutes. Remove poussins from oven and roasting tin and allow to stand while you make gravy.

Place roasting tin (without rack) over a medium heat. Add the stock, wine and vinegar and boil rapidly for a few minutes, stirring and scraping the residues off the bottom of the roasting tin, until the liquid is reduced by about half. Serve with the poussins and boiled potatoes.

Steak de Canard

This recipe works best when made with the flavourful Barbary ducks from France.

Preparation time: 1 minute
Cooking time: 11–12 minutes

4 duck breasts   *½ a lemon*
salt and pepper

Preheat grill to a medium heat. Season duck breasts with salt and pepper and grill, skin-side up, for about 6 minutes. Turn and grill for about 5 minutes on the second side, until done. (The time needed will depend on how thick the duck breasts are.)

Rub the flesh side of each breast with the cut lemon and remove from grill. Cover loosely with foil and leave to rest for a couple of minutes before serving. Serve with Sweet and Spicy Turnips (see page 85) and, if you like, a sauce made from stock, red wine and herbs.

Duck Breasts with Sun-Dried Tomatoes

Again, Barbary duck breasts are best but ordinary English duck will do, though slightly more tomato purée will be needed.

Preparation time: 5 minutes
Cooking time: 20–25 minutes, plus 5 minutes resting

1 tbsp vegetable oil   *4 bay leaves*
4 duck breasts   *salt and pepper*
2 tsp mixed dried herbs   *4 tsp sun-dried tomato purée*

As soon as you walk in the door, preheat oven to 230°C (450°F, gas 8). Brush oil on flesh side of duck breasts and sprinkle on herbs, pressing lightly to make sure it sticks. Gently lift skin of each breast and slip one bay leaf between flesh and skin. Season skin with salt and pepper.

Put breasts on a rack in a roasting tin and bake in the oven for 15 minutes. Remove from oven and spread tomato purée over each breast, then bake for another 5–10 minutes. Turn off oven, open oven door slightly and leave duck breasts to rest for 5 minutes before serving.

Roast Quail with Orange and Bacon

Some people think you need two quail per person. If you serve a hearty soup or pasta as a starter, one will be enough. Rub each bird all over with a generous pat of butter if you don't eat bacon.

Preparation time: 20 minutes
Cooking time: 25 minutes, plus 5 minutes resting

4 rashers streaky bacon
4 tbsp dry white wine or sherry
4 ovenready quail

4 tsp chopped fresh herbs (your
   choice)
1 large orange, sliced

As soon as you walk in the door, preheat oven to 230°C (450°F, gas 8). Put bacon in a bowl, cover with wine or sherry and leave to soak for 15 minutes. Rinse birds thoroughly.

Sprinkle 1 tsp herbs over each bird, then wrap each in a rasher of bacon, securing the bacon with a cocktail stick or skewer. Put orange slices in a roasting tin, put birds on top, breast-side down, and cook at the top of the oven for 12 minutes. Turn birds and cook for another 12 minutes, then remove from oven and leave to rest for 5 minutes. Put orange slices on warmed serving plates, place quail on top and serve immediately with steamed vegetables. These are also good served warm.

Pasta, Lentils and Rice

GRAINS AND PULSES are now universally recognised as among the healthiest things you can eat on a regular basis. Personally, I don't care all that much about the health angle. I love pasta, lentils and rice for the simple reason that they taste good. But it's an extra reason for eating foods that would be a pleasure to eat in any case.

PASTA

Pasta is surely the most versatile basic food around, capable of being combined with just about anything. Like many people, I have a passion for it. Incidentally, don't believe the twaddle you hear about the superiority of fresh pasta over dried. Marcella Hazan, whose books are indispensable for pasta-lovers, believes that 'High-quality factory pasta is as fine a product as the best homemade pasta'. I agree completely. Italian is the best in the world, though British-made pasta can also be good. Greek pasta is cheap, but you get what you pay for.

How to Cook Pasta

This may sound an obvious thing to say, but the first thing to do if you're cooking pasta in a hurry is to get the water boiling. That's the most time-consuming part of the operation. You can speed it up by using kettle and saucepan simultaneously, transferring each kettleful once it's boiled and refilling the kettle immediately. In the recipes that follow, I assume that you have started boiling the water before proceeding with the sauce.

Use a large saucepan as pasta absorbs almost twice its weight in water, and if there isn't enough water, your pasta won't cook properly. However, big pasta pans and stockpots are expensive, so here's a useful trick if you don't have one. Boil water in your largest saucepan *and* in the kettle. As the pasta starts cooking and the water level drops, top up the saucepan using boiling water from the kettle. You may need to do this three or four times. It's a bit of a chore, but better than having mushy pasta.

For the cooking itself, this basic technique applies to all the pasta dishes that follow:

1 Use a generous 1 litre (1¾ pints) water for every 100 g (4 oz) pasta. Get the water boiling vigorously and add around 1 tsp salt per 1 litre (1¾ pints).

2 Put the pasta in the pan all at once, give it a good stir and set a timer for 8 minutes (dried pasta) or 2 minutes (fresh). Start testing when the timer goes off; the pasta might not be done yet, but it's important not to overcook it. If the pasta isn't done, re-test every minute (for dried pasta) or every 30 seconds (for fresh) until it is.

3 When the pasta is cooked (*al dente*, as the Italians say, that is tender but still slightly firm to the bite), pour it into a colander in the sink and shake it to expedite draining. When the flow of water from the colander has slowed to a trickle, transfer the pasta either to the serving bowl or to the saucepan containing the sauce. It's not necessary to drain off all the water; water helps moisten the sauce. Stir well and serve.

How Much Pasta to Serve

I never like to say how big a portion of pasta is. It depends on three things: what else you're eating, what's in the sauce, and how hungry you are. As a ready reckoner, figure on 75–100 g (3–4 oz) for a main course, 50 g (2 oz) as a starter. But if you're as crazy about pasta as I am, nothing less than 100 g (4 oz) will do as a main course. It's always best to err on the side of excess, as leftover pasta can either be reheated or eaten at room temperature the next day. Pasta itself is not a fattening food. When calories creep in, they come from the sauce.

LENTILS AND RICE

Rice is sometimes dismissed as being boring or stodgy. But it's an excellent accompaniment and can be used – as in my Rice Salad with Prawns and Mint (see page 82) – as the basis of a delicious one-dish meal. Pulses need less argument, and lentils in particular have been 'rediscovered' by the modern generation of both French and British chefs. You're as likely to find them in posh restaurants as in vegetarian eateries.

I eat lentils with just about anything: sausages, chops, poultry or eggs. See page 43 for a recipe in which they're served with fish, a surprising but delicious combination.

Hulled lentils become mushy more easily than those that still have the hulls on, and I prefer them for this reason. Best of all are *lentilles de Puy*, tiny bluish-green lentils from France. Soaking is strictly optional, though it shortens cooking times somewhat.

The two recipes on pages 80 and 81 can be made with other pulses, including white, red or black-eyed beans. These will need overnight soaking. Increase the cooking time by 50–100 per cent, and watch the cooking liquid to make sure it isn't drying out. This takes no more trouble than cooking lentils, and the variety of good dried beans available is a boon to after-work cooks. Most beans are better the day after you cook them, and the leftovers are good as a salad or side dish for days to come.

Boiled rice is the perfect accompaniment for anything with Chinese flavours, and you can jazz it up in all sorts of ways. The basic technique for cooking rice is on page 81, followed by a pair of one-dish meals made with rice.

Fusilli alla Puttanesca

This is a simplified version of a famous Roman dish. *Puttanesca* means 'whore's style'; no one knows the origin of the name.

Preparation time: 10 minutes
Cooking time: 20–25 minutes

6 tbsp extra-virgin olive oil
3 tbsp butter
2 cloves garlic, coarsely
  chopped
100 g (4 oz) stoned black olives
½ dried red chilli, seeded and
  finely chopped, or ½ tsp
  Tabasco
1 can anchovies, drained and
  coarsely chopped

400-g (14-oz) can Italian plum
  tomatoes, drained and
  coarsely chopped
2 tbsp capers
450 g (1 lb) fusilli (spirals) or
  other short pasta
chopped fresh parsley, to
  garnish

Heat oil and butter until medium-hot in a very large frying pan. Sauté garlic for 30 seconds, then add olives, chilli or Tabasco and anchovies and sauté another minute. Add tomatoes and simmer for 15 minutes. Add capers and cook for 5 minutes more.

In the meantime, cook pasta (see page 69). When done, drain and add to sauce. Cook for 1–3 minutes, until pasta is cooked and thoroughly coated with sauce. Garnish with chopped parsley. May be served at room temperature if sauce is not too liquid. (Do *not* serve with cheese.)

Penne with Red-Hot Pesto

If sun-dried tomatoes are unavailable, double the quantity of tomato purée.

Preparation time: 15 minutes
Cooking time: 10–12 minutes

2 red peppers
2 sun-dried tomatoes or 1 tbsp
  sun-dried tomato purée
1 small dried red chilli, seeded
  and chopped
1 clove garlic, chopped
1 sprig fresh thyme or ½ tsp dried

1 tbsp tomato purée
3 tbsp olive oil
2 tbsp freshly grated Parmesan
  cheese
salt and pepper
450 g (1 lb) penne (quills) or
  other small pasta

Grill one red pepper until the skin is well blackened, then peel, seed and coarsely chop. Mix with all ingredients, except the remaining red pepper and pasta, and purée by hand or in a food processor. Seed and finely chop the remaining red pepper, then add to the pesto mixture. Cook pasta (see page 69). When cooked, drain pasta and mix with pesto. Serve immediately with extra Parmesan cheese handed round.

Chinese Sesame Noodles

This delicious dish is a good way of using up leftover chicken. If you don't have any leftovers, buy your chicken ready-cooked or poach 1–2 chicken breasts in stock (a cube is fine) for 25 minutes. Eat hot or prepare well in advance and serve as a salad. Use spaghetti or spaghettini if you can't get Chinese noodles.

Preparation time: 10–15 minutes
Cooking time: 5 minutes

150–250 g (6–8 oz) cooked
  chicken breast meat
325 g (12 oz) Chinese egg
  noodles (dried or fresh)
3 spring onions or 1 small onion,
  thinly sliced

2 red peppers, seeded and thinly
  sliced
3 large carrots, thinly sliced
100 g (4 oz) bean sprouts

Dressing

2 tbsp sesame paste (tahini)   Tabasco, to taste (optional)
6 tbsp soy sauce   1 tsp sugar
1 tbsp sesame oil   salt and pepper
3 tbsp red wine vinegar

Cut chicken into very thin slices. Combine dressing ingredients and mix well.

Cook noodles or pasta (see page 69), then drain well and toss with dressing. If serving as a salad, spread out on a large serving platter to cool, then arrange remaining ingredients on top. If serving hot, skip the cooling and serve immediately.

Pasta Disguised as a Greek Salad

Another dish that can be eaten hot, warm or at room temperature.

Preparation time: 5 minutes
Cooking time: 10–12 minutes

450 g (1 lb) short pasta   100 g (4 oz) firm black olives
4 tbsp olive oil   100 g (4 oz) feta cheese,
50 ml (2 fl oz) Greek yogurt   crumbled
1 heaped tsp dried oregano   1 can anchovies, drained and
1 large beef tomato, seeded and   chopped (optional)
  coarsely chopped   ½ crisp lettuce, shredded

Cook pasta (see page 69) and drain immediately. Toss with olive oil, yogurt and oregano and either mix in remaining ingredients or arrange them on top. If you're serving the pasta as a salad, mix while hot with the olive oil only, and wait to add the other ingredients when you're ready to eat.

Penne with Artichoke Hearts and Fennel

This dish is even better made with fresh globe artichokes. If you're feeling up to it, serve the leaves as a starter with a vinaigrette dressing and reserve the hearts for the pasta.

Preparation time: 10 minutes
Cooking time: 10–15 minutes

4 artichoke hearts, packed in oil
5 tbsp extra-virgin olive oil
1 clove garlic, finely chopped
2 large bulbs fresh fennel, thinly
    sliced
salt and pepper

325 g (12 oz) penne (quills) or
    other short pasta
juice of ½ a lemon
freshly grated Parmesan cheese
2 tbsp finely chopped fresh
    parsley

Remove artichokes from oil, drain well and coarsely chop. Heat 3 tbsp olive oil in a frying pan and add garlic and fennel. Season with salt and pepper and sauté for 10 minutes over a medium heat. While they are cooking, get pasta cooking (see page 69).

Add artichoke hearts to frying pan. Stir gently to mix, add lemon juice, then turn off heat. When pasta is cooked, drain well and toss with remaining oil and a few spoonfuls of Parmesan. Top with contents of frying pan and sprinkle with parsley. Serve immediately.

Pasta Salad with Tomatoes, Cucumber and Fresh Dill

This dish can be served either hot or cold.

Preparation time: 10 minutes
Cooking time: 10–12 minutes

450 g (1 lb) short pasta (such as
    fusilli or penne)
1½ tbsp extra-virgin olive oil
2 beef tomatoes, skinned,
    seeded and diced

½ large cucumber, seeded and
    diced
small handful fresh dill, chopped

Vinaigrette
1 tsp tomato purée   2 tbsp freshly grated Parmesan
1 tbsp extra-virgin olive oil   cheese
1½ tsp balsamic vinegar

To serve cold: Cook pasta (see page 69). Meanwhile, combine all vinaigrette ingredients. When pasta is done, drain well and toss with olive oil, then spread out on a platter to cool. Keep pasta, vegetables and vinaigrette separate until required. Just before serving, toss all ingredients together and mix in dill.

To serve hot: Gently heat tomatoes, tomato purée and cucumber in all the olive oil (2½ tbsp), then add vinegar and dill, and pour over cooked pasta. Serve Parmesan separately.

Spaghetti alla Carbonara

This ultra-simple recipe may be my favourite dish in the entire world.

Preparation time: 5–10 minutes
Cooking time: 10–12 minutes

325 g (12 oz) spaghetti   1 small onion, chopped
150 g (6 oz) streaky bacon   (optional)
   (preferably rindless)   2 large eggs
small pat butter (optional)   2 tbsp single cream (optional)
                                      freshly grated Parmesan cheese

Fill a saucepan with water, bring to the boil and cook spaghetti (see page 69). Meanwhile, cut rind off bacon, if necessary, and shred bacon into pieces about the size of matchsticks. Heat butter (if using) in a frying pan (preferably non-stick), add bacon and cook slowly for 5-10 minutes, stirring frequently. Add onion (if using) after 2–3 minutes.

Beat together eggs and cream (if using) in a bowl large enough to hold the pasta. Mix in 2 tbsp Parmesan.

When spaghetti is done, drain well and pour into bowl with egg mixture. Add bacon, toss well and serve immediately with extra Parmesan.

Pasta Shells with Mushrooms and Avocado

Preparation time: 10 minutes
Cooking time: 10–12 minutes

250 g (8 oz) mushrooms
75 ml (3 fl oz) single cream
50 ml (2 fl oz) dry white wine
1 sprig fresh thyme or large
*　pinch dried*
salt and pepper

325 g (12 oz) conchiglie
1 ripe avocado
1 tbsp balsamic or red wine
*　vinegar*
freshly grated Parmesan cheese

Wipe mushrooms with a wet kitchen paper towel and slice very thinly. Heat cream and wine very gently in a saucepan and add mushrooms and thyme. Season with salt and pepper. Cook gently for 5–8 minutes, until mushrooms are just soft but still a little firm to the bite. (This dish may be cooked in advance up to this point.)

Meanwhile, cook the conchiglie (see page 69). Cut avocado in half, remove stone and peel. Chop roughly into pieces about 1 cm (½ inch) square and toss with vinegar.

When pasta is nearly done, gently reheat mushroom mixture. Drain cooked pasta, pour into mushroom mixture and stir well to mix. Remove to a bowl and put avocado piece on top. Toss again, sprinkle with Parmesan and serve immediately.

Fusilli with Sage Butter and Parmesan Shavings

This was inspired by a dish served at the Arts Theatre Café, Great Newport Street, London W1. It couldn't be simpler, but you need fresh sage and a generous lump of good Parmesan.

Preparation time: 2 minutes
Cooking time: 10–12 minutes

325 g (12 oz) fusilli (spirals)
75 g (3 oz) butter
10 leaves fresh sage, coarsely
    chopped or torn

large chunk fresh Parmesan
    cheese
salt and pepper

Cook fusilli in boiling water (see page 69). Meanwhile, melt butter in a large saucepan, add sage and heat very gently for 3 minutes. Remove from heat.

Using a vegetable peeler, shave 16 very thin slices off the cheese. When pasta is cooked, drain and toss in sage butter. Season with salt and pepper and put on to warmed serving plates. Top each plate with shavings of cheese and serve immediately.

Spaghetti with Fresh Tomatoes

Mediterranean tomatoes have more flavour than those from Jersey, the Canary Islands and, particularly, Holland.

Preparation time: 5 minutes
Cooking time: 10–12 minutes

900 g (2 lb) ripe tomatoes
4 tbsp extra-virgin olive oil
large handful fresh herbs (such
    as basil, dill, chives or
    coriander)

salt and pepper
325 g (12 oz) spaghetti
freshly grated Parmesan cheese

If you wish to, skin tomatoes by making a small slit in each one and immersing in boiling water for 15 seconds. The skins should then come away easily.

Cut tomatoes in half and scoop out seeds and jelly. Slice tomatoes into shreds about 9 mm (⅜ inch) thick and mix well with oil, herbs and salt and pepper. If you wish, you may heat the mixture gently for a couple of minutes, just to warm it through. Cook spaghetti in boiling water (see page 69) and drain well, then toss with the sauce. Top with Parmesan and serve immediately.

Blini Linguini

This is a party dish, or something to make if you feel like pampering yourself. Linguini is a long pasta, similar to spaghetti, but fatter.

Preparation time: 10–15 minutes
Cooking time: 15–20 minutes

250 g (8 oz) salmon steak or fillet
15 g (½ oz) butter
1 small onion, finely chopped
225 ml (8 fl oz) sour cream or
  crème fraîche

1 tbsp dry white wine
325 g (12 oz) linguini
4 tbsp lumpfish roe (optional)

Skin salmon and cut into thin shreds or small dice. Melt butter in a large saucepan and gently cook onion for 5–10 minutes, until soft. Add sour cream or *crème fraîche* and wine, and simmer gently for 1 minute. (The dish may be prepared in advance up to this point.)

Cook linguini in boiling water (see page 69) and bring onion and cream mixture to a gentle heat. When pasta is done, drain it and add to the onion and cream with the salmon pieces. Stir gently so the salmon doesn't break up; the heat of the pasta will cook the salmon. Divide pasta between warmed serving plates and top with 1 tbsp lumpfish roe (if using). Serve immediately.

Penne with Red Peppers and Aubergines

This simple recipe is a little time-consuming for one evening's cooking, but the sauce can be made up to 24 hours in advance.

Preparation time: 30 minutes
Cooking time: 10–15 minutes

2 red peppers
2 large aubergines
few drops vegetable oil (optional)
3 tbsp extra-virgin olive oil

2 spring onions, cut into 5-cm
  (2-inch) shreds
2 cloves garlic, chopped
2 tbsp sun-dried tomato purée

50 ml (2 fl oz) dry white wine
small handful fresh herbs or your
    choice, chopped

325 g (12 oz) penne (quills) or
    other short pasta
freshly grated Parmesan cheese
    (optional)

Preheat oven to 230°C (450°F, gas 8). Put whole peppers and aubergines in a baking dish with a few drops vegetable oil (if using). Bake at top of oven for about 30 minutes, turning once, until their skins are blackened. Leave to cool.

Heat olive oil in a large saucepan and gently cook onions and garlic for 1 minute. Add tomato purée and wine and simmer for another 3 minutes.

Peel aubergines and peppers and cut into 5-cm (2-inch) shreds. Add to saucepan with herbs and mix well.

Cook pasta in boiling water (see page 69) and bring sauce to a gentle heat. When pasta is done, drain, mix with sauce and serve immediately with Parmesan cheese (if using).

Fusilli with Smoked Chicken and Chicory

Preparation time: 5 minutes
Cooking time: 10 minutes

1 smoked chicken breast or leg
2 heads chicory
450 g (1 lb) fusilli (spirals) or
    other short pasta
50 g (2 oz) butter

salt and pepper
50 ml (2 fl oz) single cream or
    Greek yogurt
freshly grated Parmesan cheese
    (optional)

Bone chicken and cut into chunks or slices about 5 mm (¼ inch) thick. (You may skin chicken if you're watching calories.) Trim chicory and separate the leaves, then slice into shreds about the same thickness as the chicken.

Cook pasta in boiling water (see page 69). Meanwhile, heat butter in a frying pan and gently cook chicory. When it's good and soft, turn off heat and mix in chicken. Season with salt and pepper and pour in the cream or yogurt. Pour over cooked and drained pasta and serve immediately with Parmesan cheese, if using.

Basic Lentils

These lentils can be puréed the next day to make soup, or eaten cold with yogurt as a salad.

Preparation time: 5 minutes
Cooking time: 20–40 minutes

250 g (8 oz) lentils
1–2 tbsp olive oil
1 small onion, finely chopped
1 clove garlic, finely chopped
2 small carrots, finely chopped
1 bay leaf

1 tsp dried oregano or mixed
* dried herbs*
400 ml (14 fl oz) water or stock,
* plus extra as needed*
salt and pepper

Wash lentils and remove any bad ones. Heat oil in a heavy saucepan and sweat vegetables and herbs for a few minutes, then add lentils. Stir to coat with oil, then add water or stock. Simmer for 20–40 minutes, until soft. (Cooking time depends on the type of lentil used and whether or not they're presoaked.) You may need to add more water or stock if the lentils are drying out. Season with salt and pepper.

Variation

Add a small can (about 200 g/7 oz) Italian plum tomatoes, drained and coarsely chopped, with the lentils. Reduce water or stock to 300 ml (½ pint).

Lentils with Sausages

This turns Basic Lentils (left) into a main course.

Preparation time: 5 minutes
Cooking time: 20–40 minutes

150 g (6 oz) strong-flavoured precooked sausage (such as chorizos,
   louganikas, kielbasa*)*
ingredients for Basic Lentils (left)

Cut sausage into 1-cm (½-inch) chunks. Follow recipe for
Basic Lentils and, when lentils are nearly cooked, add
sausage and continue cooking for about another 5 minutes,
just to heat through.

Basic Rice

Rice is better measured by volume rather than weight.
Don't use the quick-cook type; it's not as good.

Preparation time: 1 minute
Cooking time: 20–25 minutes

long-grain rice to fill a measuring   *350 ml (12 fl oz) water*
   jug to the 225-ml (8-fl oz) mark   *1 tsp salt*

Put rice in a saucepan and add water and salt. Bring to the
boil and boil (not too vigorously) for 2 minutes. Cover
tightly, turn the heat down very low and cook, without
removing the lid, for 20 minutes.

Check the rice to see if it's done; the grains should be
cooked right through but should retain just a hint of 'bite'. If
the rice isn't ready, cover and cook for another 3–5 minutes.
When it's done, stir the rice with a fork to separate the
grains and either serve immediately or leave with the lid on
for up to 20 minutes.

One-Pot Chicken and Rice Dinner

If you make this for guests, you'll need to do it in a flameproof casserole.

Preparation time: 5 minutes
Cooking time: 30–35 minutes

2 tbsp vegetable oil
2 cloves garlic, finely chopped
2.5-cm (1-inch) cube fresh root ginger, peeled and finely chopped
1 tbsp medium curry powder
4 chicken breasts or legs

1 medium onion, sliced into 5-cm (2-inch) pieces
long-grain rice to fill a measuring jug to the 250-ml (8-fl oz) mark
350 ml (12 fl oz) water
250 g (8 oz) French beans

Heat oil in a heavy saucepan and add garlic, ginger and curry powder. Stir-fry over medium heat for 1 minute, adding a few drops of water if mixture sticks. Push contents to one side of pan and add chicken, making sure it's touching the bottom of the pan. Cook for 2 minutes on each side (4 minutes on each side if you like chicken well-done), to brown lightly.

Add onion to pan and cook, stirring, for 2 minutes more. Add rice and water, bring to the boil, then cover and simmer for 20 minutes. Add beans, *without stirring*, and cook for another 5 minutes. If rice gets too dry, add more water.

Rice Salad with Prawns and Mint

This is a good way of using up leftover cooked rice.

long-grain rice to fill a measuring jug to the 225-ml (8-fl oz) mark or the equivalent amount of cooked rice
1 tbsp extra-virgin olive oil

250 g (8 oz) frozen peas
350 g (12 oz) prawns, preferably raw
4 tbsp Vinaigrette (see page 120)
small handful fresh mint leaves

If cooking rice in advance, proceed as in Basic Rice recipe (page 81), but add oil to rice before stirring. Remove from saucepan and spread out to cool on a platter.

Cook peas according to the instructions on the packet, then drain well and cover. If using raw prawns, cook in rapidly boiling salted water for 1 minute (or steam for 5 minutes), until just done. Leave to cool, then cover and refrigerate until needed. Toss all ingredients with vinaigrette, mix in mint and serve immediately.

Vegetables and Salads

THERE ARE MORE RECIPES in this book for vegetables than for any other single category of food. I am not a vegetarian, obviously, but I do love vegetables, and the variety of recipes in this chapter indicates why: they're so enormously versatile. Some of the recipes, such as Stir-Fried Courgettes with Red Onion (see page 88), are clearly side dishes. Others, such as Baked Potatoes with Mozzarella and Double Tomatoes (see page 86), would make a main course as filling and satisfying as any meat or fish dish.

It's impossible to give comprehensive buying tips in a short space, but a few general points are essential. First, look carefully at whatever vegetable you're buying – and handle it first before deciding whether to take it home. Fresh vegetables should be firm, bright in colour, and free of dried or wrinkled patches. Second, be guided by the market – and modify recipes accordingly. If you want to make Fennel Salad with Caerphilly and Pine Nuts (see page 95) but there's no fennel in the market, buy another vegetable (such as red peppers) and use that instead. Third, and most happily, if you see a vegetable you've never cooked before, buy it and experiment. There is now a greater variety of vegetables around than ever before. What seems mysterious today may be your favourite next week.

Sweet and Spicy Turnips

Preparation time: 5 minutes
Cooking time: 25–30 minutes

675 g (1½ lb) medium turnips, cut
   into 5-mm (¼-inch) slices
25 g (1 oz) butter
1 tsp ground cinnamon

1 tsp cayenne
1 tbsp clear honey
1 tsp cumin seeds

As soon as you walk in the door, preheat oven to 180°C (350°F, gas 4). Blanch turnip slices in boiling salted water for 4 minutes, then drain. Butter a heavy baking or gratin dish and put in one layer of turnips. Sprinkle on cinammon and cayenne. Put in remaining turnips, brush with honey and sprinkle with cumin. Bake in oven for 25–30 minutes. Brown under grill for 2 minutes if turnips look too pale.

Potato and Onion Gratin

Preparation time: 20 minutes
Cooking time: 30–40 minutes

675 g (1½ lb) King Edward
   potatoes, peeled and cut into
   3-mm (⅛-inch) slices
1 medium Spanish onion,
   coarsely chopped

salt and pepper
450 ml (¾ pint) milk or rich stock
butter (optional)

Preheat oven to 200°C (400°F, gas 6). Place a layer of potatoes in a shallow ovenproof dish. Add a layer of onion and season lightly with salt and pepper. Repeat until all potatoes and onion are finished, then pour on milk or stock. Dot with butter (if using) and bake, uncovered, in the oven for 30–40 minutes.

To microwave: Cover and cook at full power for 12 minutes. Leave to rest for 5 minutes, then brown under the grill.

Variation

Sprinkle grated Parmesan cheese on each of the potato and onion layers.

Baked Potatoes with Mozzarella and Double Tomatoes

Preparation time: 15 minutes
Cooking time: 45 minutes–1 hour

4 baking potatoes
2 very red tomatoes, peeled, seeded and cut into 5-mm (¼-inch) dice
2 tbsp finely chopped sun-dried tomatoes
2 tbsp chopped fresh basil or 1 tbsp dried
1 Mozzarella cheese, finely diced
salt and pepper
freshly grated Parmesan cheese

Preheat oven to 230°C (450°F, gas 8) and bake potatoes for 30–40 minutes, until just cooked. Cut potatoes in half lengthways and scoop out pulp to within 5 mm (¼ inch) of skins. Break up pulp and mix with tomatoes, basil and Mozzarella. Season with salt and pepper and return to skins. Sprinkle lightly with Parmesan and bake in oven for another 15–20 minutes, until cheese has melted to a nice gooey consistency and the top is browned.

Baked Potatoes with Salsa Verde y Blanca

Preparation time: 5 minutes
Cooking time: 30–40 minutes

4 large baking potatoes
225 ml (8 fl oz) Greek yogurt
3 tbsp chicken stock
1 green or red pepper (or some of both), seeded and finely chopped
small handfuls fresh parsley and coriander, finely chopped
½ fresh green chilli, seeded and finely chopped

Preheat oven to 230°C (450°F, gas 8) and bake potatoes for 30–40 minutes, until just cooked. In the meantime, make salsa by mixing all other ingredients. When potatoes are done, cut them open and spoon a quarter of the salsa over each one. Serve immediately.

Stir-Fried Parsnips

Preparation time: 10 minutes
Cooking time: 10–12 minutes

An unusual treatment for an underrated vegetable. Small parsnips work best.

450 g (1 lb) parsnips
2 tbsp sultanas
2 tbsp vegetable oil
1 tsp finely chopped fresh ginger

salt and pepper
4 tbsp chicken stock or water
1 tbsp lemon juice

As soon as you walk in the door, boil a kettle of water. Peel parsnips, cut out their woody cores and slice about 9 mm (⅜ inch) thick. Soak sultanas in boiling water for 5 minutes, then drain and set aside.

Heat oil in a wok or frying pan, add parsnips, ginger and salt and pepper, and stir-fry for 2–3 minutes, until parsnips take on a bit of colour. Turn heat down to medium-low and add stock and sultanas. Cover and cook for 3–6 minutes, until parsnips are fully cooked. Add lemon juice, mix well and serve immediately. A good accompaniment to grilled or roasted meats.

Roasted Vegetable Cups

Preparation time: 10–15 minutes
Cooking time: 30–40 minutes

4 large red peppers
25 g (1 oz) butter
2 small onions, finely chopped
8 large mushrooms, thinly sliced

4 tbsp extra-virgin olive oil
1½ tbsp finely chopped fresh
   basil or parsley
salt and pepper

As soon as you walk in the door, preheat oven to 200°C (400°F, gas 6). Cut tops off peppers and remove seeds. Tear off four double pieces of foil about 30.5 cm (12 inches) square and smear the centres with butter. Stand a pepper on the buttered area of each piece, then fill with onions and mushrooms. Dribble on oil and season with herbs, salt and pepper. Pull up foil at corners, taking care not to tear it, and twist together over tops of peppers to seal. Cook in centre of oven for 30–40 minutes. Serve hot or warm.

Stir-Fried Courgettes with Red Onion

The onion is cooked by the residual heat in the pan, which must have a tight-fitting lid.

Preparation time: 10 minutes
Cooking time: 3–4 minutes

450 g (1 lb) courgettes
3 tbsp olive oil
salt and pepper

1 red onion, thinly sliced
150 ml (6 fl oz) good stock
2 tbsp chopped fresh herbs

Cut courgettes in half, then lengthways into pieces about 1 cm (½ inch) thick. Heat oil until very hot in a wok or frying pan. Add courgettes, season with salt and pepper, and fry, stirring constantly, for about 90 seconds. Turn heat off and lay onion slices on top. Now, very quickly, pour on stock and cover pan. Do not remove the lid, even if it sounds like a volcano is erupting inside the pan! Leave for 2 minutes, then remove lid and scatter herbs on top. This dish is good hot or at room temperature.

Steamed Baby Vegetables with Rosemary Butter

Good baby vegetables are delicious. Treat them simply.

Preparation time: 2 minutes
Cooking time: 5–10 minutes

25 g (1 oz) unsalted butter
1 small clove garlic, finely
chopped

1 tsp dried rosemary
450 g (1 lb) mixed baby
vegetables

Melt butter in a small saucepan and cook garlic and rosemary very gently for 1 minute. Remove from heat and set aside for 1 hour to allow flavours to infuse.

Steam vegetables for 5–10 minutes, until cooked but still very firm to the bite. Put in a warmed serving dish and keep warm. Gently reheat rosemary butter for a few seconds, then strain on to the vegetables. Serve immediately.

Grilled Potatoes

A non-fat alternative to chips.

Preparation time: 3 minutes
Cooking time: 35–40 minutes

450 g (1 lb) 'waxy' potatoes (such as Maris Bard)

Gently steam or boil potatoes for 25–30 minutes, until barely cooked. Peel, if you wish, then slice 1 cm (½ inch) thick. Grill under a hot grill for 3–5 minutes per side, until nicely browned. You can cheat and brush on a little olive oil or melted butter, but it's really not necessary. Serve with Tomato Sauce (see page 121) or with lemon wedges.

Stir-Fried Cauliflower with Fennel Seeds

This is based on a soup recipe given to me by chef Carla Tomasi of Frith's restaurant, London W1. To make it as soup, simply use 1.1 litres (2 pints) water and purée the mixture in a blender when the vegetables are soft.

Preparation time: 5 minutes
Cooking time: 6–8 minutes

1 medium cauliflower	100 ml (4 fl oz) water
2 tbsp olive oil	salt and pepper
1 tbsp fennel seeds	3 tbsp chopped fresh parsley or
½ tsp ground turmeric	coriander

Break cauliflower into florets, keeping some of the green outer leaves, and wash under running water. Heat oil in a wok or large frying pan until sizzling hot. Add fennel seeds and fry for 1 minute, stirring constantly. Add cauliflower and turmeric, cook for a few seconds, then add water and bring to the boil. Season with salt and pepper, lower heat to medium and simmer for 4–6 minutes, until cauliflower has lost its crunchiness but is still firm to the bite. Stir in parsley or coriander and serve immediately.

Aubergine and Pepper Salad with Chilli Vinaigrette

This is a little bit time-consuming but exceptionally tasty. It's equally good as a vegetarian main course or as part of a summer buffet lunch.

Preparation time: 10 minutes
Cooking time: 20–30 minutes

1 red and 1 yellow pepper	6 tbsp safflower oil
2 large black aubergines, about	2 tbsp wine vinegar
675 g (1½ lb) total weight	1 tbsp lemon juice
1 green chilli, seeded and finely	1 large handful fresh coriander
chopped	leaves, chopped, to garnish

Grill peppers until their skins are blackened all over, then peel, seed and cut into very narrow strips.

While peppers are grilling, cook aubergines either in a steamer or in the microwave (see below). If steaming, lay directly in the steamer and cook for about 20 minutes, until soft.

Mix chilli with oil, vinegar and lemon juice, preferably in a blender. When aubergines are completely cool, cut or tear into thin strips and lay on a platter. If not serving immediately, cover tightly with clingfilm. Just before serving, lay the peppers on top of the aubergines. Whisk the chilli vinaigrette again and spoon it over. Garnish with coriander and serve.

To microwave: Prick aubergines all over and lay them on a plate. Microwave at full power for 12–13 minutes, then remove and allow to cool.

Baked Potato Cake

Preparation time: 3 minutes
Cooking time: 30–40 minutes

1 quantity Perfect Mashed
Potatoes (see page 98)

225 ml (8 fl oz) milk
50 g (2 oz) butter

Preheat oven to 230°C (450°F, gas 8). Mix potatoes with milk and spread out evenly in a pie or quiche dish. (If preparing in advance, film top with extra milk to prevent discolouring.)

Dot potato with butter and bake at centre of oven for 30–40 minutes, until top has a nice brown crust. (May sit in warm oven for up to 15 minutes before serving.)

Potato Galettes

These are easy to make for up to eight people, and a real treat for yourself when dining alone on a cold winter evening.

Preparation time: 10–15 minutes
Cooking time: 25–40 minutes

4 medium baking potatoes   salt and pepper
4 large pats butter

Peel potatoes, trimming them well, and slice as thin as you can get them, about 3 mm (⅛ inch) thick. Melt one pat butter in a frying pan large enough to hold a quarter of the potato slices in a neat circle of overlapping layers. Arrange slices in pan and turn heat up so butter is sizzling just a little bit. Season with salt and pepper and cook for about 5 minutes, until the galette is brown on the bottom. Turn, season and cook for a further 2–4 minutes, until the underside is brown. Remove from pan and repeat to make another three galettes. Eat with chops or eggs.

Onion 'Spaghetti'

The name is misleading, but the dish – ribbons of Spanish onion, gently sautéed and tossed in oil or melted butter and freshly grated Parmesan – is inexpensive and delicious. Serve as a starter or side dish with chops – or as a topping for pasta.

Preparation time: 5 minutes
Cooking time: 15–20 minutes

1 large Spanish onion   2 tbsp freshly grated Parmesan
1 tbsp extra-virgin olive oil   cheese
                                        15 g (½ oz)butter (optional)

Slice onion into thin disks about 3 mm (⅛ inch) thick. Stack the disks and, placing the knife tip at the centre of the stack, cut down as if you were making the first cut in a pie. Separate the discs into broken rings.

Heat oil in a frying pan and gently sauté onions for 15–20 minutes, until they're soft and mild in flavour, but still have a bit of 'bite'. (They can happily sit in the pan for 10 or 15 minutes at this point.)

Reheat onions, if necessary, then remove to a warmed serving bowl. Toss with Parmesan cheese and butter (if using) and serve immediately.

Stir-Fried Cabbage with Thai Flavours

Cabbage is particularly useful during winter months when the selection of home-grown vegetables is unexciting. This simple dish reheats well, and can be used as the basis for soup the next day.

Preparation time: 15 minutes
Cooking time: 15 minutes

1 tbsp olive or vegetable oil
250 g (8 oz) white or red
   cabbage (see **Note**), shredded
4-cm (1½-inch) cube fresh root
   ginger, peeled and finely
   chopped

1 small clove garlic, finely
   chopped
2.5-cm (1-inch) piece fresh
   lemongrass, finely chopped
salt and pepper
100 ml (4 fl oz) chicken or
   vegetable stock

Heat oil in a wok or large frying pan, add cabbage, ginger, garlic and lemongrass and stir-fry for a minute or so, tossing well to spread the oil evenly. Season well with salt and pepper, pour in stock, cover and cook at a medium heat for 10–15 minutes, stirring thoroughly at least three times.

If you like, you can turn heat right down and let cabbage bubble away for up to 40 minutes – but check occasionally to make sure liquid isn't cooking away. This will produce a softer result which is no less delicious.

Note: It's hard to find a cabbage weighing less than 450 g (1 lb) or so. Make double the recipe, or save the uncooked cabbage, tightly wrapped, in the vegetable compartment of your fridge. It will keep happily for several days.

If using red cabbage, add 1 tbsp red wine vinegar and 2 tbsp red wine to help it keep its colour.

Three-Layer Salad with Chinese Vinaigrette

There's no reason to stop eating salad in winter. This one arranges cooked vegetables in layers, and any combination may be used. An attractive starter, salad or light weekend lunch.

Preparation time: 10 minutes
Cooking time: 20 minutes

2 green peppers
2 red peppers
four 1-cm (½-inch) slices from a
   large onion
2 tbsp vegetable oil
4 slices good bread or toast
   (optional)

Vinaigrette
1 tsp sesame oil
2 tbsp vegetable oil
1 tsp soy sauce
1 tbsp red wine vinegar
salt and pepper

Grill peppers until blackened all over, then peel off skins, cut in half lengthways and remove seeds. Combine all ingredients for vinaigrette. Fry onion in a non-stick pan with a little oil until browned and tender. Turn carefully to keep slices whole, and don't worry if they blacken slightly: the black bits are delicious.

Just before serving, assemble on plates with bread (if using) on the bottom. Brush generously with vinaigrette and serve. You or your guests should cut into the salad with a knife and fork so that each mouthful contains a piece of each vegetable.

Smoky Lentil Salad with Orange Segments

This versatile recipe can be made with smoked trout, salmon, halibut, chicken, ham or duck. The important thing is to get the right contrast of fresh and smoky flavours. This is a good way of using up leftover lentils, though it's simple to cook them to order (see page 80).

Preparation time: 15 minutes
Cooking time: none if lentils are already cooked; 40 minutes if you're cooking them specially for the dish

large handful mixed salad leaves
  (such as oak leaf and frisée)
2 stalks celery
2 shallots or spring onions
100 g (4 oz) cooked brown
  lentils, cooled (see page 80)

2 tbsp Vinaigrette (see page 120)
150 g (6 oz) smoked fish or meat
2 small oranges, peeled and
  segmented

Wash and dry salad leaves thoroughly. Slice celery 5 mm (¼ inch) thick. Cut shallots or spring onions into fine shreds. Toss lentils, onions and celery with vinaigrette.

Arrange salad leaves on serving plates and put a spoonful of lentils on each plate. Cut smoked fish or meat into thin strips or shreds about 1 cm (½ inch) across. Lay orange slices, followed by smoked fish or meat, neatly on top of lentils and serve.

Fennel Salad with Caerphilly and Pine Nuts

When buying fennel, look for smooth heads with no hint of dryness in the outer layers.

Preparation time: 10–15 minutes
Cooking time: 2 minutes

a few handfuls mixed salad
  leaves
2 small heads fennel (each about
  the size of your fist)
75 g (3 oz) young Caerphilly
  cheese

25 g (1 oz) pine nuts
2 tsp finely chopped fresh basil
  or tarragon (optional)
2 tbsp Vinaigrette made with
  extra-virgin olive oil (see page
  120)

Wash and dry salad leaves thoroughly, then tear into very small pieces. Top and tail fennel, cut out the cores, and slice as thinly as possible. Arrange fennel slices on four plates and divide the salad leaves between them. Crumble cheese on to each plate.

Just before you're ready to serve, put the pine nuts in a small dry frying pan and heat gently over a medium heat until they're a pale toasty brown. Remove from pan and scatter over salads, followed by herbs (if using). Dribble vinaigrette over each salad and serve immediately.

Hob-Roasted New Potatoes

If you wish to cut down the 'roasting' time, parboil the potatoes in rapidly boiling water for 10 minutes, then drain well before putting them into the hot fat.

Preparation time: 3 minutes
Cooking time: 20–30 minutes

675 g (1½ lb) new potatoes
2 tbsp vegetable oil or chicken fat
salt and pepper

Clean potatoes and heat oil or fat in a large, lidded frying pan or shallow flameproof casserole. Add potatoes, rolling them around to coat with oil, then season with salt and pepper. Cover and cook over a slow but steady heat, stirring or shaking the pan from time to time. The aim is to brown the skins all over without making them too crisp. This is actually easy to do as long as you stir or shake the potatoes occasionally while they are cooking. Potatoes about 5 cm (2 inches) wide will take 30 minutes or so; smaller spuds will take much less time.

Sautéed Mushrooms with Indian Spices

Use more cayenne and pepper if you like very spicy food.

Preparation time: 15 minutes
Cooking time: 5–8 minutes

450 g (1 lb) fresh mushrooms
5 tbsp corn or peanut
   (groundnut) oil
1 tsp ground cumin
1 tsp ground coriander
¼ tsp cayenne
1 'tsp black pepper
1 bay leaf, broken in half

1 tbsp finely chopped fresh root
   ginger
1 small clove garlic, finely
   chopped
salt
sprigs fresh coriander or parsley,
   to garnish

If mushrooms are large, cut in half or quarter. Heat oil in a large frying pan and stir-fry dry spices and bay leaf for 30 seconds. Add ginger and garlic and stir-fry for another minute. Add mushrooms and sauté, stirring several times, for 3–5 minutes, until they're cooked but still firm. Season with salt. Drain off excess liquid, if necessary, and garnish with coriander or parsley. Serve either hot or warm.

Braised Chicory

Preparation time: 2 minutes
Cooking time: 1–1½ hours

4 large heads chicory
juice of ¼ lemon
2 tbsp butter (strictly optional)

about 600 ml (1 pint) chicken or
   vegetable stock

Preheat oven to 180°C (350°F, gas 4). Put chicory heads in a baking dish just large enough to hold them in one layer. Add lemon juice and dot with butter (if using). Add enough stock to come about three quarters of the way up the chicory. Cover with foil and cook in the oven for 1–1½ hours.

To microwave: Use 100 ml (4 fl oz) stock for two heads. Cover tightly and cook at full power for 7–8 minutes.

Perfect Mashed Potatoes

Use 'floury' potatoes, such as King Edward, Maris Piper or Pentland Crown.

Preparation time: 2 minutes
Cooking time: 25–30 minutes

450 g (1 lb) 'floury' potatoes, peeled
100–200 ml (4–7 fl oz) milk or stock
butter or extra-virgin olive oil

Cut potatoes into pieces roughly the same size (about 4 cm/1½ inches is ideal). Put them in a large saucepan and add cold water to a depth of 2.5 cm (1 inch) over tops of spuds. Bring to the boil, reduce the heat to its lowest point, and simmer gently for about 25 minutes, until just done. To test, a small, sharp knife should slide easily right into the centre of a spud.

Drain potatoes well, then return to the saucepan and leave to stand for a minute or so, until the last of the cooking water has evaporated. Mash potatoes well with a ricer or masher, then gradually pour in milk or stock. Stir constantly as you pour so the liquid is spread right through the purée. You can tell you've added enough when the mixture slides easily off the spoon. Now add butter (if using milk) or oil (if using stock). You can add as much as you want, depending on how calorie-conscious you're feeling. 1 tbsp per 450 g (1 lb) potatoes will do, but let's face it: the more you add, the more wickedly delicious your potatoes will be! Cooked this way, the potatoes can sit happily, covered, for several hours.

Party Menus

GIVING DINNER PARTIES after work is easy if you keep the food simple. The ten menus in this chapter aim at simplicity which sacrifices nothing in the way of good flavour. The main dishes are more complicated than those in the rest of this book, but by no means excessively so; for most of the cooking time, the dishes look after themselves.

When giving dinner parties, planning becomes even more important. Do the preparation and cooking as far in advance as possible so you'll have time to spare in the countdown to the party. And if you are put off entertaining by the thought that the food must look beautiful, remember that your guests don't want to sit and admire pretty pictures on the plate before them. What they want is honest food that tastes good. Presentation should respect the forms and colours of the basic ingredient, letting the food speak for itself.

MENU ONE – AN INFORMAL BASH

Guacamole (see page 20)
Jambalaya
Pastry-less Apple Tart (see page 114)

Jambalaya

Like paella, which it resembles, Jambalaya is a flexible dish. The only essential ingredients are rice, spices and vegetables; the rest is up to you. This recipe serves 4–8 people, depending on what else you're having and how hungry you all are.

Preparation time: 5–10 minutes
Cooking time: 30–35 minutes

250 g (8 oz) smoked sausage, preferably Polish kielbasa (optional)
1 large onion
2 green or red peppers, seeded
4 stalks celery
6 tbsp vegetable oil
1 quantity Cajun Spice Mix (see page 124)
2 bay leaves

2 cloves garlic, finely chopped
8 chicken drumsticks or 4 chicken breasts, each cut in half
325 g (12 oz) long-grain rice
2 tbsp tomato purée
800 ml (28 fl oz) chicken or fish stock
450 g (1 lb) firm-fleshed fish (monkfish would be ideal)

Cut sausage, onion, peppers and celery into 2.5-cm (1-inch) pieces. Heat oil in a large flameproof casserole and cook sausage gently for 2 minutes, then add spices, bay leaves, vegetables and garlic. Cook over a medium heat for 4–5 minutes, stirring frequently.

Add chicken to casserole and cook for 2 minutes more, then add rice, tomato purée and stock. Stir well to mix, then cover and cook over a low heat for about 20 minutes, until nearly done.

Finally, add fish and cook for about 5 minutes, until just done. Serve with a small green salad.

MENU TWO – A COLD WINTER NIGHT

Curried Vegetable Soup (see page 22)
Stuffed Cabbage *or* Roast Beef with Yorkshire Pudding
Baked Bananas (see page 113)

Stuffed Cabbage

Use pork, beef or lamb. The reheated leftovers are delicious.

Preparation time: 20 minutes
Cooking time: 1 hour

1 Savoy or white cabbage
50 g (2 oz) butter
2 medium onions, finely chopped
2 medium carrots, finely
  chopped
450 g (1 lb) lean meat (pork,
  beef or lamb), minced
100 g (4 oz) long-grain rice

1 tsp ground cinnamon
1 tbsp ground coriander
salt and pepper
300 ml (½ pint) Tomato Sauce
  (see page 121)
450 ml (¾ pint) beef or chicken
  stock

Bring a large saucepan of salted water to the boil and
preheat oven to 180°C (350°F, gas 4). Core cabbage and
carefully remove 12 leaves. Blanch in boiling water for
about 10 minutes, until soft. Drain well. Finely chop two
more cabbage leaves.

Heat butter in a saucepan or frying pan, add onions,
carrots and chopped cabbage, cover and sweat for 3
minutes, then add meat, rice and spices. Season with salt
and pepper and cook for 5 minutes, breaking meat into
small lumps. Stir in Tomato Sauce and simmer gently for 5
minutes more. Roll 2–3 heaped tbsp meat into each cabbage
leaf, firmly tucking in ends. Place in a buttered ovenproof
dish, pour on stock and cover with foil. Bake in the oven for
about 40 minutes, basting two or three times.

Roast Beef and Yorkshire Pudding

Use rolled forerib or topside. If you're eating this *à deux*, the leftovers will make two or three additional meals.

Preparation time: 5 minutes
Cooking time: 30 minutes–1 hour

*900 g–1.4 kg (2–3 lb) joint of
   roasting beef
½ tsp mixed dried herbs
½ tsp freshly ground black
   pepper*

*½ tsp salt
2 tbsp vegetable oil
1 quantity Toad in the Hole
   batter (see page 40)*

If possible, remove joint from fridge 1 hour before cooking. Mix herbs, pepper and salt and rub into meat. Preheat oven to 230°C (450°F, gas 8). Heat oil in a frying pan until very hot, add meat and brown all over. Drain off excess fat and put joint in a roasting tin. Cook in the centre of the oven for 12 minutes per 450 g (1 lb) (rare), 15 minutes per 450 g (1 lb) (medium-rare), 18 minutes per 450 g (1 lb) (medium). Remove to a serving platter, cover loosely with foil, and leave for 25 minutes. Do not turn off oven.

While beef is resting, make Yorkshire pudding. Either in the roasting tin or in individual Yorkshire Pudding (popover) tins, heat a bit of dripping from the roast or an equivalent amount of vegetable oil. When it's smoking hot, pour in batter and cook in the centre of the oven while the beef is resting. As soon as the pudding has risen and is browned, remove from oven and serve with beef.

MENU THREE – AN ELEGANT DINNER PARTY FOR FOUR

This time-consuming meal is definitely for weekends only. However, two of the dishes are served cold, and nearly all of the work can be done in advance.

No-Cook Bloody Mary Soup (see page 25)
John Burton-Race's Skate Salad with Soy Sauce
Clafoutis (see page 116)

Skate Salad with Soy Sauce

This is a much-simplified version of a famous dish created by John Burton-Race, chef-patron of L'Ortolan in Shinfield, Berkshire. He recommends baby spinach, radicchio and curly endive for the salad.

Preparation time: 30–40 minutes
Cooking time: 30 minutes

2 skate wings, each about
    550 g (1¼ lb)
2 medium carrots
2 medium courgettes
salt and pepper
225 ml (8 fl oz) fish or vegetable
    stock
1 shallot, finely chopped
    (optional)

small bunch chives, finely
    chopped (optional)
4 tbsp Vinaigrette (see page 120)
few drops soy sauce
325 g (12 oz) mixed salad leaves
juice of ½ a lemon
2 tomatoes, peeled, seeded and
    cut into 5-mm (¼-inch) dice
    (optional)

Place skate on a heatproof dish or plate that will fit comfortably in your steamer. Cut carrots and courgettes in julienne strips or slice them thinly. Scatter over the skate, season with salt and pepper, and steam for 10 minutes, turning once. Remove from steamer and allow fish to cool, reserving vegetables and cooking liquid.

While waiting for fish to cool, carefully pour cooking liquid into a small saucepan and add fish or vegetable stock. Bring to the boil and boil rapidly until reduced by half. Add shallot and chives (if using) to Vinaigrette, plus a few drops of soy sauce.

Toss salad leaves with vinaigrette and arrange on four plates. Cut fish off bone and slice into 2.5 cm (1 inch) pieces. Arrange skate around salad, season with lemon juice and sprinkle on vegetables and tomatoes (is using). Warm in the oven for a few moments, then serve immediately.

MENU FOUR – A ROMANTIC DINNER À DEUX

Salad of Marinated and Smoked Salmon (see page 15)
Rack of Lamb with a Mustard and Parmesan Crust
Grilled Nectarines (see page 119)

Rack of Lamb with a Mustard and Parmesan Crust

The rack of lamb (also known as best end of lamb) should be chined, that is the bone should be cut through to make carving easier. If you're buying from a supermarket, this should have been done already. If buying from a butcher, ask for it to be done.

Preparation time: 10 minutes
Cooking time: 25 minutes plus 5 minutes resting

1 rack of lamb, made up of
  6 cutlets
1 tbsp Dijon Mustard
1 tbsp corn or sunflower oil
1 tbsp finely chopped fresh
  parsley

handful of breadcrumbs or finely
  crushed Weetabix
1 tbsp freshly grated Parmesan
  cheese
salt and pepper

Preheat oven to 200°C (400°F, gas 6). Cut off fat and scrape off meat from the end of each cutlet bone, leaving 2.5 cm (1 inch) of bare bone at the end of each cutlet.

Mix all other ingredients and spread evenly over the lamb. Place lamb on a rack in a roasting tin and roast for 25 minutes. Turn off oven, open the door, and leave lamb to stand for 15 minutes before carving. Serve with baked or sautéed potatoes and green beans.

MENU FIVE – ORIENTAL FLAVOURS

Thai-Style Steamed Eggs (see page 17)
Fishy Gumbo with Ginger and Spring Onion
Fresh fruit

Fishy Gumbo with Ginger and Spring Onion

This is a variation of a Cajun-style gumbo. Use any seafood or firm-fleshed fish, and don't neglect cheap but flavourful types like huss and gurnard.

Preparation time: 15–20 minutes
Cooking time: 25–30 minutes

2 small green or red peppers, seeded
3 stalks celery
4 large or 8 small spring onions
50 ml (2 fl oz) vegetable oil
25 g (1 oz) plain white flour
1 clove garlic, finely chopped

2.5-cm (1-inch) cube fresh root ginger, peeled and chopped
salt
350 ml (12 fl oz) fish, chicken or vegetable stock
675 g (1½ lb) mixed fish or seafood, cleaned and cut into bite-sized pieces

Chop all vegetables into 5-mm (¼-inch) dice. In a large flameproof casserole, heat oil until medium-hot and add flour a spoonful at a time, stirring constantly with a wooden spoon. When it has reached a peanut colour, add vegetables, garlic and ginger, and mix well. Season with salt, stir again to mix, then pour in stock, bring to the boil and simmer for 15 minutes. The dish may be prepared in advance up to this point.

Add fish or seafood to casserole and simmer for about 5 minutes, until barely done. Skim visible oil from surface and serve immediately with boiled rice or potatoes and steamed vegetables.

MENU SIX – CHEAP AND CHEERFUL
Sweet Pepper Tortilla (see page15)
Herby Meat Loaf
Stir-Fried Summer Fruits (see page 114)

Herby Meat Loaf

Use at least three herbs for maximum complexity of flavour;
serve with lemon wedges.

Preparation time: 10 minutes
Cooking time: 1 hour

2 eggs
675 g (1½ lb) coarsely minced
    beef, pork or chicken
1 tbsp Cognac (optional)
2 tbsp Worcester sauce
4 tbsp chopped mixed fresh
    herbs (parsley, coriander,
    thyme, tarragon, rosemary,
    etc.)

1 tsp ground cumin
1 medium onion, finely chopped
1 clove garlic, finely chopped
3–4 rashers unsmoked bacon
salt and black pepper

Boil eggs for about 4 minutes, until hard enough to peel
without breaking the whites, but still soft on the inside.
Plunge them into cold water and peel carefully.

Preheat oven to 180°C (350°F, gas 4). Mix meat with
other ingredients, except bacon, and season with salt and
pepper. Put about a third of the mixture in a small loaf tin.
Place eggs in centre of dish and carefully spoon in more
meat to surround them. Put the rest of the mixture on top,
followed by the bacon rashers, and bake for 1 hour. Serve
hot or at room temperature.

MENU SEVEN – A VEGETARIAN DINNER

No-Cook Cucumber Soup (see page 26)
Aubergine Parmigiana
Berry Compote with Basil (see page 115)

Aubergine Parmigiana

Preparation time: 30 minutes
Cooking time: 1 hour 20 minutes

675 g (1½ lb) aubergines
salt and black pepper
3 tbsp olive oil
350 ml (12 fl oz) Tomato Sauce
(see page 121)

150 g (6 oz) Italian Mozzarella
cheese, coarsely chopped
3 tbsp freshly grated Parmesan
cheese

Preheat oven to 180°C (350°F, gas 4). Cut aubergines lengthways into slices about 5 mm (¼ inch) thick. Sprinkle with salt and place in a colander for 30 minutes. Rinse and pat dry.

Brush each aubergine slice with oil and grill or fry for about 3 minutes each side, until lightly browned. Lightly oil a baking or gratin dish and put in a layer of aubergines. Spread on a layer of tomato sauce, followed by a layer of Mozzarella. Season with plenty of black pepper. Continue until ingredients are used up and sprinkle on the Parmesan. Bake in the oven for 35–40 minutes or until the top is bubbling and brown. Allow to stand for a few minutes before serving.

MENU EIGHT – FOR FISH FANATICS

Smoked Fish 'Pâté' (see page 16)
Fish and Potato Pie
Berry Wine Soup (see page 117)

Fish and Potato Pie

Use any good white fish, or a combination of fresh and smoked fish; add some peeled prawns to make an extra-special pie.

Preparation time: 40–45 minutes
Cooking time: 40 minutes

450 g (1 lb) 'floury' potatoes (such as King Edward or Maris Piper)
250 g (8 oz) button mushrooms
2 green peppers, seeded
1 medium onion, coarsely chopped
2 tbsp dry white wine or vermouth

350 ml (12 fl oz) milk
1 clove
1 bay leaf
450 g (1 lb) mixed smoked and fresh white fish
small handful fresh parsley, chopped
salt and pepper
butter

Boil potatoes in skins for about 20 minutes, until barely cooked, then peel and slice thickly. Preheat oven to 200°C (400°F, gas 6).

Slice mushrooms, peppers and onion 3 mm (⅛ inch) thick and cook gently in the wine or vermouth in a non-stick frying pan for about 5 minutes, until just softened. Remove from pan and set aside.

Place milk, clove and bay leaf in frying pan. Heat gently, add fish and simmer very gently for 5 minutes. Remove fish, skin it, and flake with a fork. Strain cooking liquid and reserve. Put fish and cooked vegetables in a shallow casserole, sprinkle with parsley, season with salt and pepper, and pour on about half the milk in which fish was cooked. Cover with potato slices and dot with butter. Bake for 40 minutes, until liquid in pie is bubbling enthusiastically.

MENU NINE – COMFORT FOOD

Cabbage Soup with Almonds (see page 25)
Shepherd's Pie or Serious Macaroni Cheese
Eve's Pudding (see page 118)

Shepherd's Pie

Preparation time: 20 minutes
Cooking time: 1 hour

450 g (1 lb) Perfect Mashed
   Potatoes (see page 98)
1 tbsp vegetable oil or 15 g
   (½ oz) butter
1 large onion, coarsely chopped
100 g (4 oz) mushrooms,
   coarsely chopped
2 large carrots, coarsely
   chopped

450 g (1 lb) minced or shredded
   beef or lamb
1 tsp mixed dried herbs
400-g (14-oz) can Italian plum
   tomatoes, drained, seeded
   and coarsely chopped
150 ml (¼ pint) red wine
150 ml (¼ pint) beef stock
butter

While potatoes are boiling (see page 98), heat oil or butter
in a large frying pan or small flameproof casserole and add
vegetables. Cook over a gentle heat for 5 minutes, then add
meat and herbs. Continue cooking, breaking up any lumps
of meat, for 5 minutes more.

Add tomatoes to the pan with wine and stock. Simmer,
uncovered, for 20–25 minutes, until meat is cooked and liquid reduced by about 50 per cent. (If it's still too watery, stir
in about 1 tbsp flour.)

While mixture is cooking, preheat oven to 190°C (375°F,
gas 5). When meat is ready, tip it into a baking dish and
spread potatoes evenly over the top. Dot with butter and
cook in the oven for 20–25 minutes, until spuds are a pale
golden brown. Allow to rest for 5 minutes before serving.
Nice with a watercress salad.

Serious Macaroni Cheese

Don't laugh! This dish is for grown-ups, not the nursery.

Preparation time: 20 minutes
Cooking time: 30 minutes

50 g (2 oz) butter
100 g (4 oz) ham or smoked
* bacon, chopped (optional)*
1 small onion, finely chopped
1 clove garlic, finely chopped
325 g (12 oz) macaroni
2 tbsp double cream
150 g (6 oz) crumbly Chèvre
* cheese*
50 g (2 oz) grated Gruyère
* cheese*

4 tbsp freshly grated Parmesan
* cheese*
salt and pepper
cayenne
2 tbsp finely chopped fresh
* parsley*
grated rind of 1 lemon
4 tbsp dried breadcrumbs
600 ml (1 pint) milk

Preheat oven to 220°C (425°F, gas 7). Melt butter in a small frying pan and gently sauté ham or bacon (if using) for 1 minute (ham) or 3 minutes (bacon). Add onion and garlic and sauté until translucent.

Cook macaroni in plenty of boiling water (see page 69). While it's cooking, mix cream, Chèvre, Gruyère and half Parmesan. Season with salt, pepper and a good pinch of cayenne. In another bowl, mix parsley, lemon rind, bread-crumbs and remaining Parmesan.

When pasta is just cooked, drain well and mix with cheese and bacon mixtures. Pour into a buttered ovenproof dish, add milk, and sprinkle parsley mixture on top. Bake for 20 minutes and serve with a green salad.

MENU TEN– SUMMER LUNCH FOR FOUR OR FORTY

Aïoli
Berry Compote with Basil (see page 115) or fresh fruit

Aïoli

Aïoli may be the only dish in the world that's named after the sauce that goes with it. The sauce is a mayonnaise that contains a mind-boggling amount of garlic. Served as a dip, it makes one of the best summer meals you can imagine. To complete the meal, serve a number of other dips from the selection on pages 122–124. Either way, this is a meal in itself, and requires no accompaniment. (For those who prefer to avoid eating raw egg yolks, an Aïoli recipe using cooked eggs is given on page 124.)

A dip-based meal accommodates vegetarians and non-vegetarians alike. Everyone takes a plate and helps him- or herself. If they don't eat meat, they can simply leave it on the serving plate. For a large-scale dip-based meal, I would suggest any or all of the following:

hard-boiled eggs;
raw carrots, cauliflower, cucumber, celery, fennel, tomatoes (cherry if you can find them);
a good selection of salad greens, including chicory;
cold steamed leeks;
raw mushrooms marinated lightly in olive oil and lemon;
steamed new potatoes with skins on;
red and yellow peppers, either grilled or raw, seeded and sliced;
courgette and aubergine slices fried in extra-virgin olive oil;
a good selection of breads and breadsticks

If you want something meaty, serve cold rare roast beef sliced very thin, or cold roast chicken.

Preparation time: 10 minutes for the Aïoli, 30—40 minutes for the vegetables, etc.
Cooking time: anything from 20 minutes to 1 hour, depending on how much food you're preparing

10 cloves garlic   *2 tsp French mustard*
1 tsp salt   *225 ml (8 fl oz) each of olive oil*
2 egg yolks   *and vegetable oil*
juice of 2 lemons

If you wish, the garlic may be tamed by boiling the cloves in plenty of salted water for 20 minutes. Drain and dry well, then proceed as follows:

Pound garlic or chop finely and put in a food processor or blender with salt, egg yolks, lemon juice and mustard. Blend for 1 minute, then turn off machine. Put oils together in a jug. Turn processor on again and pour oils through the feed tube in a thin, steady stream. As the mixture starts to thicken, you may pour more freely. Turn off machine as soon as mixture is thickened.

Puddings

THIS CHAPTER is a short one for the simple reason that most people don't eat puddings in the course of an ordinary evening at home. Occasionally we all deserve a treat, however, and a sweet dish at the end of a meal is one such treat. If you have a sweet tooth, why reach for biscuits or a chocolate bar after dinner at home, when a few extra minutes would produce Baked Bananas (below) or Grilled Nectarines (see page 119) instead? They really do taste better than a bar of chocolate! And they're better for you.

Baked Bananas

Preparation time: 5 minutes
Cooking time: 25 minutes

4 ripe bananas
4 tbsp fresh orange juice
2 tsp Cointreau (optional)

2 tsp sugar (optional)
2 tsp ground cinnamon
butter

As soon as you walk in the door, preheat oven to 200°C (400°F, gas 6). Peel bananas and slice each one lengthways, almost (but not quite) cutting them in half. Sprinkle the insides with orange juice, Cointreau (if using), sugar (if using) and cinnamon, then put the two halves of each banana together, wrap in squares of buttered foil and seal. Bake on the top shelf of the oven for about 25 minutes, until soft. Serve in the foil with cream (optional).

Stir-Fried Summer Fruits

Preparation time: 15 minutes
Cooking time: 5 minutes

900 g (2 lb) hard summer fruits (such as apples, pears, peaches, apricots)
25 g (1 oz) butter
15 g (½ oz) sugar (or to taste)
juice of ½ a lemon

250 g (8 oz) mixed berries (such as raspberries, loganberries, strawberries)
2 tbsp Calvados or Cointreau (optional)

Peel and core or stone hard fruits and slice about 5 mm (¼ inch) thick. Heat butter in a frying pan or wok until just bubbling. Add fruit and sugar and stir-fry gently for 2 minutes, then add lemon juice and toss well to mix. Add berries, toss gently, then put in liqueur (if using) and ignite to burn off alcohol. Serve immediately with yogurt, cream or *crème fraîche*. Other toppings, such as raisins or chopped nuts, can be added if you wish.

Pastry-less Apple Tart

Preparation time: 10–15 minutes
Cooking time: 30–40 minutes

8 firm eating apples (such as Cox or Granny Smith)
50 g (2 oz) butter

juice of 1 lemon
2 tsp ground cinnamon
25 g (1 oz) sugar

As soon as you walk in the door, preheat oven to 230°C (450°F, gas 8). Peel and core apples and slice lengthways into 6–8 pieces. Heat butter in a shallow flameproof casserole and toss in apples with lemon juice and cinnamon.

Sprinkle sugar over and cook in the oven for 30–40 minutes, until top is golden brown.

The tart may be served hot, warm or at room temperature, with good vanilla ice cream on the side. It also goes well with slices of mature Cheddar.

Berry Compote with Basil

Use any combination of strawberries, raspberries, currants, loganberries, blueberries, blackberries and bilberries. Cherries and apricots would also be nice.

Preparation time: 5 minutes
Cooking time: 3–4 minutes, plus about 1 hour cooling

450 g (1 lb) fresh berries
25 g (1 oz) caster sugar
juice of 1 large orange

few drops vanilla essence or
½ a vanilla pod
1 tbsp Grand Marnier (optional)
4 or 5 leaves fresh basil

Wash, dry, stone, hull and stem berries, as necessary, and place in a bowl. Gently heat sugar, orange juice, vanilla and Grand Marnier (if using) in a saucepan for 3–4 minutes, until sugar dissolves. Pour over fruit, mix well and refrigerate, stirring from time to time so the juice is evenly distributed.

Just before serving, remove vanilla pod, if necessary. Tear basil into small pieces and toss with berries. Serve with *fromage frais* if you wish.

Easy Strawberry Cream Tarts

Use bought pastry or make your own – it's actually very simple if you have a food processor.

Preparation time: 20 minutes (using bought pastry)
Cooking time: 20–25 minutes

450 g (1 lb) shortcrust pastry
200 ml (7 fl oz) double cream
100 ml (4 fl oz) milk

450 g (1 lb) strawberries, hulled
2 tbsp sugar (optional)

Preheat oven to 200°C (400°F, gas 6). Roll out pastry into four small rounds or two larger ones, each about 3 mm (⅛ inch) thick. If you wish to, make a lattice from one round (or two if using the smaller size).

Put pastry rounds on a non-stick baking sheet, prick all over with a fork, and bake in the upper third of the oven for 10–15 minutes, until pastry is a light golden brown. Transfer to a wire rack to cool.

When ready to serve, whip cream and milk together and slice strawberries about 1 cm (½ inch) thick. Spread cream over the base of each tart, then top with strawberries. Put the top of the tart lightly on each one. Sprinkle with sugar (if using) and serve immediately.

Clafoutis

This French classic is one of the simplest of all puddings. The version here doesn't use as much sugar as most recipes, but I don't think the extra sweetness is necessary. It can also be made with halved plums or apricots.

Preparation time: 5–20 minutes
Cooking time: 30–40 minutes, plus at least 20 minutes cooling

450 g (1 lb) cherries
25 g (1 oz) caster sugar
75 g (3 oz) plain flour

2 eggs, beaten
¼ tsp salt
250 ml (8 fl oz) milk

As soon as you walk in the door, preheat oven to 180°C (350°F, gas 4). Stone cherries (optional) and mix with half the sugar. Spread out evenly in a lightly buttered shallow baking dish. Mix remaining ingredients with remaining sugar to make a batter and pour over fruit. Bake in the oven for 30–40 minutes, until batter is nicely browned. Cool to room temperature before serving. Sprinkle on extra sugar if you want to.

Berry Wine Soup

This recipe is inspired by one in Pierre Koffmann's *Memories of Gascony* (Pyramid). You can adjust the sweetness by adding sugar and varying the type of wine used. I would suggest a medium-dry Vouvray or a sparkling wine. If you have a drier wine, use more sugar. If the wine is sweet, no extra sugar will be needed.

Preparation time: 10 minutes, plus 1–1½ hours marinating

450 g (1 lb) fresh berries (such as raspberries, loganberries, strawberries)

1 tbsp crème de cassis
caster sugar, to taste
375 ml (half a bottle) white wine

Clean and hull berries and chop in half (or quarters if very large). Mix gently in a bowl with the *crème de cassis* and a sprinkling of sugar, then refrigerate for up to 1 hour. Pour the wine into the bowl and refrigerate for another 30 minutes, then serve in bowls with extra sugar and single cream (if desired). A grinding of black pepper adds a surprisingly delicious accent!

Simple Bavarian Cream with Berries

A proper Bavarian cream (also called *Bavarois)* is made with custard, whipped cream and gelatine. This simplified version dispenses with the custard for a lighter result, and takes all of 15 minutes to make. Use any berry you want, except gooseberries.

Preparation time: 15 minutes, plus 3–4 hours chilling

75 ml (3 fl oz) ruby port or water
1 tbsp gelatine
250 g (8 oz) fresh berries (such as raspberries, loganberries, strawberries)

150 ml (¼ pint) double cream
100 ml (4 fl oz) milk
1 tbsp sugar (or to taste)

Heat port or water in a small saucepan *without boiling.* Remove from heat, pour in gelatine and stir until dissolved. Clean and hull berries and put in a blender or food processor. Add dissolved gelatine and blend until smooth. Put mixture through a sieve for a finer result, though this is not necessary.

Whip cream and milk together until almost trebled in volume. Add sugar and whisk again briefly, then whisk in berry mixture just to blend. Don't worry if the mixture is streaked with colour. Put in a clean bowl and chill for 3–4 hours. Serve with sponge fingers or butter cookies, or as a topping for fruit salad.

Eve's Pudding

You can flavour steamed and baked puddings with all sorts of things. This one, adapted from *The Dairy Book of British Food* (Ebury Press), uses chopped apples. Using 2 large tablespoons marmalade or honey instead would make the dish even easier.

Preparation time: 20 minutes
Cooking time: 1 hour

250 g (8 oz) eating apples, peeled, cored and roughly chopped
1 tsp ground cinnamon
150 g (6 oz) self-raising flour

pinch of salt
75 g (3 oz) softened butter
50 g (2 oz) caster sugar
1 egg, beaten
100 ml (4 fl oz) milk

Preheat oven to 180°C (350°F, gas 4). Butter a baking dish. Mix the apple with the cinnamon, then spread over the bottom of the baking dish. In a mixing bowl, mix the flour, salt, butter and sugar. Add the egg and mix it in, then slowly add the milk. Pour into the baking dish and bake for about 1 hour, until the pudding is well risen. To serve, turn the dish out on to a warmed platter. Serve with single cream or custard.

Grilled Nectarines

You could also use peaches, apricots or even good eating apples like Cox's Orange Pippin or Discovery.

Preparation time: 2 minutes
Cooking time: 8–10 minutes

4 ripe nectarines
1 tbsp sugar

Preheat grill for a couple of minutes while you cut the nectarines in half and remove the stones. Put fruit, cut-side up, in a roasting tin and add a little water – just enough to moisten the bottom of the tin. Sprinkle sugar on top of fruit, making sure every bit is covered. (Use more, if necessary.) Place under grill and cook at a medium heat for 8–10 minutes, until sugar is nicely browned and the flesh soft. Serve immediately with cream, Greek yogurt, or *crème fraîche*.

Sauces, Dips and Spice Mixes

Basic Vinaigrette

I don't like giving recipes for vinaigrette. Unless you go to a lot of trouble combining tiny amounts of many different ingredients – and some chefs and cookery writers do that, very successfully – you're dealing with a very simple proposition. Opposite is the simple proposition, just for the record.

Bear in mind, however, that this is only the basis of salad dressing. The range of additional flavours is endless, from fresh or dried herbs to mustard, garlic, capers, olive paste, sun-dried tomatoes, soy sauce, ginger – almost any season-ing you can think of. When you start experimenting, there's an infinite variety of vinaigrette tricks. This is one of the pleasures of salad-making.

Even with a plain vinaigrette made from only oil and vinegar, you can produce a wide range of variations. Using less vinegar will produce a milder result, more vinegar a sharper one. Buy different oils – extra-virgin olive, sesame and walnut, as well as plain vegetable oils – and different vinegars, such as sherry and balsamic. (Malt vinegar has its uses, but salad dressing is not one of them.) Most supermarkets sell a good selection. And oil and vinegar are not the only bases for salad dressing. Try chicken stock or low-fat yogurt instead of all or part of the oil for a lighter result, or a teaspoon of cream for a richer one.

Ideally you should never make salad dressing in the same way twice. Look in your larder and think, "What can I do that's different?"

Preparation time: 1 minute

3 parts oil
1 part wine vinegar
salt and pepper

Combine ingredients and mix well. If you eat a lot of salad, it's worth making enough for a couple of weeks and storing it, tightly covered, in the fridge. If you do this, add pepper just before serving. I use a combination of peanut (groundnut) oil and extra-virgin olive oil, but you should experiment and find your own preference.

Tomato Sauce

Fresh tomatoes are often flavourless, even when they're supposed to be at their best, so I tend to use canned Italian plum tomatoes instead. This recipe makes enough sauce to serve with 450 g (1 lb) pasta. Make double or triple the quantity (no extra effort) and freeze some in plastic containers.

Preparation time: 10 minutes
Cooking time: 25–35 minutes

1–2 tbsp extra-virgin olive oil
2 tbsp finely chopped onion
2 tbsp finely chopped carrot
2 tbsp finely chopped celery
1 clove garlic, finely chopped
¼ tsp each dried oregano, sage and tarragon

1 tsp chopped fresh parsley or basil
400-g (14-oz) can Italian plum tomatoes
1 tbsp tomato purée
salt and pepper

Heat oil in a saucepan and gently cook vegetables and garlic for 3 minutes. Add herbs and stir in. Drain tomatoes and break up with a knife, then add to saucepan with tomato purée. Season with salt and pepper. Cook, stirring occasionally, for 20–30 minutes, until sauce is thick. For a finer texture, put through a sieve or purée in a blender or food processor. The dried herbs can be varied to your taste.

Gazpacho Salsa

This salsa may be made in advance.

Preparation time: 10 minutes
Cooking time: 15–20 minutes

2 red peppers
4 large, ripe beef tomatoes,
    skinned, seeded and coarsely
    chopped
1 small onion, finely chopped
4 thick slices good-quality white
    bread, crusts removed,
    soaked in water and squeezed
    dry

1 cucumber, peeled, seeded and
    coarsely chopped
100 ml (4 fl oz) extra-virgin olive
    oil
100 g (4 oz) firm black olives,
    stoned and finely chopped
salt and pepper

Steam, grill or microwave peppers until really soft. Remove skin and seeds and chop finely. Put tomatoes, onion, bread and cucumber in a food processor and blend until nearly perfectly smooth. (If you don't have a food processor, put ingredients through a mouli, or chop them by hand as fine as you can get them.) Mix in a bowl with red pepper and oil. Add more bread if too thin, more oil if too thick. Stir in olives and season with salt and pepper.

Variation

Add one small green chilli, seeded and finely chopped.

Tex-Mex Salsa

This recipe is adapted from the cookery book of the Junior League of Austin, Texas. The quantities given here work perfectly, but they can all be varied almost infinitely to suit your taste, or a particular dish. If you don't want salsa to be scorchingly hot, remove seeds from chillies before chopping.

Preparation time: 10 minutes, plus 1–2 hours standing (optional)

450 g (1 lb) ripe tomatoes
1 medium onion or 3 spring
   onions, finely chopped
4 small green chillies, finely
   chopped

1½ tsp cumin seeds
juice of 1 lemon
handful fresh coriander or Italian
   parsley, finely chopped
salt and pepper

Chop tomatoes in 1-cm (½-inch) pieces. Combine ingredients, adding plenty of pepper, in a glass or ceramic bowl and leave to stand for 1–2 hours, if possible, tossing occasionally.

Stilton Dip

Serve this dip with crudités (raw vegetables), toast or breadsticks. It can be made well in advance, if necessary.

Preparation time: 2 minutes

250 g (8 oz) Stilton cheese,
   crumbled
250 g (8 oz) cottage cheese
3 tbsp extra-virgin olive oil

milk
3 tbsp finely chopped chives
black pepper

Mix the cheeses in a food processor or with a large fork until they're smooth. Add oil and mix in well, then dribble in enough milk to produce a creamy consistency. (This can be as little as a few tablespoons.) Stir in chives and season with pepper.

Hard-Boiled Aïoli

A variation on the main Aïoli recipe (see page 111), for those who don't like eating raw egg.

Preparation time: 5–10 minutes

2 cloves garlic
2 hard-boiled egg yolks
150 ml (¼ pint) extra-virgin olive
   oil

1 tbsp white wine vinegar
salt and pepper

Put garlic through a press or pound to a fine paste in a mixing bowl. (If you don't like too strong a garlicky taste, the cloves may be boiled first in their skins for 5 minutes, then drained well and peeled.)

Force egg yolks through a fine sieve and slowly add oil, whisking in as you pour. Add vinegar and blend thoroughly. Season with salt and pepper. If the consistency is too runny, add more egg yolk or a few cubes of white bread, soaked in water and then squeezed dry. If making this in advance (and it will sit in the fridge very happily for several hours), whisk again before serving as the yolks and oil will separate.

Cajun Spice Mix

This recipe was provided by David Wilby of London's Rock Island Diner, who got it from the renowned Cajun chef Beany Macgregor. Adjust proportions to suit your taste and the requirements of the dish. Use it to season grilled or sautéed meat, and see pages 44 and 58 for recipes.

Preparation time: 1 minute

1 tbsp sweet paprika
1–2 tbsp salt
1 tsp garlic powder
1 tsp onion powder
½ tsp cayenne

¾ tsp black pepper
¾ tsp white pepper
½ tsp dried thyme
½ tsp dried oregano

Combine ingredients and mix well.

Index

aïoli, 111–12
  hard-boiled aïoli, 124
apples: Eve's pudding, 118
  pastry-less apple tart, 114–15
artichoke hearts, penne with fennel
  and, 74
aubergines: aubergine and pepper
  salad, 90–1
  aubergine Parmigiana, 107
  penne with red peppers and,
  78–9
avocado: avocado with creamed
  smoked salmon, 20
  guacamole, 20–1
  pasta shells with mushrooms
  and, 76

bacon: bacon and eggs with fresh
  herbs, 41
  spaghetti alla carbonara, 75
bananas, baked, 113–14
Bavarian cream with berries,
  117–18
beef: hamburgers, 36–9
  'instant' chilli, 33
  Japanese-style beef rolls, 36
  oven-fried steak, 35
  roast beef and Yorkshire
  pudding, 102

shepherd's pie, 109
steak *frites*, 31
berry compote with basil, 115
berry wine soup, 117
blini linguini, 78
bruschetta, 19
butter, to clarify, 54

cabbage: sausages in a nest of, 34–5
  soup with almonds, 25
  stir-fried with Thai flavours, 93
  stuffed cabbage, 101
Cajun smothered chicken, 58–9
Cajun spice mix, 124
carrots: fish steaks on a bed of, 53
  soup with ginger and spring
  onion, 27
cauliflower, stir-fried with fennel
  seeds, 90
ceviche, 17–18
cheese: aubergine Parmigiana, 107
  baked potatoes with Mozzarella,
  86
  cheeseburgers, 37
  fennel salad with Caerphilly,
  95–6
  melted Stilton sandwiches, 21
  serious macaroni cheese, 110
  Stilton dip, 123

fusilli with sage butter and
    Parmesan shavings, 76–7
cherries, clafoutis, 116
chicken, 55
    baked chicken wings, 56
    baked chicken with yogurt, 59
    basic roast chicken, 56–7
    Cajun smothered chicken, 58–9
    chicken 'boulangère', 57
    chicken with Indian spices, 62
    chicken with mushrooms and
        garlic, 61–2
    Chinese sesame noodles, 72–3
    la fausse poule au pot, 60
    fusilli with smoked chicken and
        chicory, 79
    hot and sour chicken with citrus
        shreds, 60–1
    leftover chicken with peppers, 63
    marinated chicken thighs, 62–3
    one-pot chicken and rice dinner,
        82
    Provençale chicken, 64–5
    sesame chicken salad, 64
    stir-fried with ginger and spring
        onion, 58
chicory: braised chicory, 97
    fusilli with smoked chicken and,
        79
chilli: 'instant' chilli, 33
    Tex-Mex salsa, 123
Chinese sesame noodles, 72–3
chtchi, 23–4
clafoutis, 116
cod: grilled with herb crust, 47–8
    Simon Hopkinson's poached cod
        with salsa verde, 43
cotelettes Pojarski, 53–4
courgettes, stir-fried with red
    onion, 88
cucumber: no-cook soup, 26
    pasta salad with tomatoes, fresh
        dill and, 74-5
curried vegetable soup, 22–3

dips: aïoli, 111–12
    Stilton dip, 123
duck, 55
    duck breasts with sun-dried
        tomatoes, 66–7
    steak de canard, 66

eggs: bacon and eggs with fresh
    herbs, 41

baked eggs, 18
hard-boiled aïoli, 124
spaghetti alla carbonara, 75
spring onion tortilla, 14
Thai-style steamed, 17
equipment, 11
Eve's pudding, 118

la fausse poule au pot, 60
fennel: fennel salad with
    Caerphilly and pine nuts, 95–6
    penne with artichoke hearts and,
        74
fish, 42–54
    blackened fish, 44
    ceviche, 17–18
    cotelettes Pojarski, 53–4
    fish and potato pie, 108
    fish fillets 'pipérade', 51
    fish roll-ups with spinach and
        spring onion, 43–4
    fish steaks on a bed of carrots, 53
    fishy gumbo with ginger and
        spring onion, 105
    quick-baked fish fillets with wine
        and mushrooms, 50–1
    see also cod, salmon etc.
fruit: Bavarian cream with berries,
    117–18
    berry compote with basil, 115
    berry wine soup, 117
    stir-fried summer fruits, 114
fusilli: fusilli alla puttanesca, 71
    fusilli with sage butter and
        Parmesan shavings, 76–7
    fusilli with smoked chicken and
        chicory, 79

garlic, aïoli, 111–12
gazpacho salsa, 122
guacamole, 20–1

hamburgers, 36–9
herby meat loaf, 106
honey-and-spice roasted poussins,
    65

jambalaya, 100
Japanese-style beef rolls, 36
John Dory with orange cream, 50

lamb: lamb and leek stir-fry, 40
    quick-braised lamb with herbs de
        Provence, 34

rack of lamb with a mustard and parmesan crust, 104
stir-fry lamb with radicchio and chicory, 32–3
lemon broth with rice, 28
lentils, 70
　basic lentils, 80
　lentils with sausages, 81
　smoky lentil salad, 94–5
linguini, blini, 78

macaroni cheese, 110
mackerel in white wine, 45
mayonnaise, aïoli, 111–12
meat, 30–41
　herby meat loaf, 106
　stuffed cabbage, 101
　see also beef, lamb *etc*.
menus, 99–112
mushrooms: chicken with garlic and, 61–2
　pasta shells with avocado and, 76
　quick-baked fish fillets with wine and, 50–1
　sautéed with Indian spices, 97
　simple Chinese broth, 28–9
mussels: mussels with ginger and spring onion, 47
　vegetable soup with, 24

nectarines, grilled, 119
noodles, Chinese sesame, 72–3

onions: onion 'spaghetti', 92–3
　stir-fried courgettes with red onion, 88
orange segments, smoky lentil salad with, 94–5

parsnips, stir-fried, 87
party menus, 99–112
pasta, 68–70
　pasta disguised as a Greek salad, 73
　pasta salad wtih tomatoes, cucumber and fresh dill, 74–5
　pasta shells with mushrooms and avocado, 76
　see also fusilli, penne *etc*.
pâté, smoked fish, 16
penne: with artichoke hearts and fennel, 74
　with red-hot pesto, 72

with red peppers and aubergines, 78–9
peppers: aubergine and pepper salad, 90–1
　fish fillets 'pipérade', 51
　leftover chicken with, 63
　penne with red-hot pesto, 72
　penne with red peppers and aubergines, 78–9
　quick-braised pork chops with garlic and red peppers, 32
　squid with three peppers, 46
　sweet pepper *tortilla*, 15
pesto, penne with red-hot, 72
pork chops, quick-braised with garlic and red peppers, 32
potatoes: baked potato cake, 91
　baked potatoes with Mozzarella and double tomatoes, 86
　baked potatoes with *salsa verde y blanca*, 86
　chicken 'boulangère', 57
　fish and potato pie, 108
　grilled potatoes, 89
　hob-roasted new potatoes, 96
　perfect mashed potatoes, 98
　potato and onion gratin, 85
　potato galettes, 92
　shepherd's pie, 109
　steak *frites*, 31
poultry, 55–67
poussins, honey-and-spice roasted, 65
prawns, rice salad with mint and, 82–3
Provençale chicken, 64–5
puddings, 113–19

quail, roast with orange and bacon, 67

red kidney beans: 'instant' chilli, 33
red mullet with wilted watercress, 48
rice, 70–1
　basic rice, 81
　jambalaya, 100
　lemon broth with, 28
　one-pot chicken and rice dinner, 82
　salad with prawns and mint, 82–3

salads: aubergine and pepper with chilli vinaigrette, 90–1

fennel with Caerphilly and pine
  nuts, 95–6
marinated and smoked salmon,
  15–16
pasta disguised as a Greek salad,
  73
pasta with tomatoes, cucumber
  and fresh dill, 74–5
rice with prawns and mint, 82–3
sesame chicken, 64
skate with soy sauce, 103
smoky lentil with orange
  segments, 94–5
three-layer with Chinese
  vinaigrette, 94
salmon: avocado with creamed
  smoked salmon, 20
blini linguini, 78
marinated, 52
salad of marinated and smoked
  salmon, 15–16
sandwiches, melted Stilton, 21
sauces: gazpacho salsa, 122
Tex-Mex salsa, 123
tomato sauce, 121–2
sausages: lentils with, 81
sausages in a nest of cabbage,
  34–5
toad in the hole, 40–1
seafood ragoût with lemon grass,
  49
sesame chicken salad, 64
shepherd's pie, 109
shopping, 9–10
skate salad with soy sauce, 103
smoked fish 'pâté', 16
sole: fish roll-ups with spinach and
  spring onion, 43–4
soups, 22–9
spaghetti: spaghetti alla carbonara,
  75
with fresh tomatoes, 77
spice mix, Cajun, 124
spinach: chtchi, 23–4
fish roll-ups with spring onion
  and, 43–4
spring onion tortilla, 14
squid with three peppers, 46

steak, oven fried, 35
steak de canard, 66
steak frites, 31
Stilton dip, 123
strawberry cream tarts, 115–16

taramasalata, 13–14
tarts: easy strawberry cream tarts,
  115–16
pastry-less apple tart, 114–15
Tex-Mex salsa, 123
Thai-style steamed eggs, 17
toad in the hole, 40–1
tomatoes: baked potatoes with
  Mozzarella and, 86
duck breasts with sun-dried
  tomatoes, 66–7
gazpacho salsa, 122
no-cook Bloody Mary soup, 25–6
pasta salad with cucumber, fresh
  dill and, 74–5
penne with red-hot pesto, 72
spaghetti with fresh, 77
Tex-Mex salsa, 123
tomato sauce, 121–2
tomato soup with basil croûtons,
  29
tortilla, 14–15
turnips, sweet and spicy, 85

vegetables, 84
aïoli, 111–12
curried vegetable soup, 22–3
jambalaya, 10
roasted vegetable cups, 88
soup with mussels, 24
steamed baby vegetables with
  rosemary butter, 89
see also cabbage, tomatoes etc.
  and salads
vinaigrette, basic, 120–1

watercress: cream soup, 26–7
red mullet with wilted, 48
wine: berry wine soup, 117

yogurt, baked chicken with, 59
Yorkshire pudding, 102